147 Fun Things To Do In SAN ANTONIO

D1715723

written by
Karen Foulk

INTO FUN, COMPANY
PUBLICATIONS
A Division of Into Fun, Inc.
Sugar Land, Texas

147 Fun Things To Do In San Antonio

by Karen Foulk

Cover and Map illustrations by Delton Gerdes
Book Layout by Brockton Publishing

Library of Congress Catalog Card Number:
00 134556

ISBN 0-9652464-9-3

INTO FUN, INC.
P.O. Box 2494, Sugar Land, Texas 77487-2494
Phone: 281-980-9745 Fax: 281-494-9745

This book contains descriptions including operating times
and admission costs of many of the fun and interesting
places in the San Antonio area. Although a great deal of
effort has gone into making this book as up-to-date and
accurate as possible, changes constantly occur. There-
fore, before visiting a destination, please call to confirm
the information provided herein. Neither Into Fun, Co.
Publications, a division of Into Fun, Inc., the owner, nor
the author warrant the accuracy of the information in
this book which includes but is not limited to price
changes, addresses, names, hours of operation, manage-
ment or conditions of the attraction described.

Dedication

With all my love,
To my husband, Don,
who thinks I'm having too much fun.

Michael & Amber
Rachel & John
David
Rebecca

Acknowledgments

Again in appreciation for their contributions,
to the many dear friends, family members,
and associates who make this book possible.

To my husband and children,
for putting up with a busy mom.

To Jerrie Hurd my sister. Read her new book
Hoopsnaked.

To Brocky Brown of Brockton Publishing Co.
who makes it all happen.

To Merrill Littlewood, my accountant. He's the best.

To Michael Foulk, for being N2Fun's webmaster.

To Ken Barrow, for his legal help and advice.

To Annette Hruska, for designing the Into Fun car

To Sharon Cooper, always a friend.

Writing this book was fun. In fact, it's been so much fun, when I call it work my husband laughs.

But this book will make it easy for you. Everything you need to know about San Antonio—for great family adventures—is at your fingertips. Simply choose from the following for fun things to do, terrific places to stay, and delightful places to eat.

San Antonio has wonderful restaurants and I've gone to a lot of trouble to find the best ones. I think you'll enjoy any I've mentioned in the book. Of course, you haven't experienced San Antonio until you've tasted their Tex-Mex cuisine. Plan to eat lots of tasty Mexican food.

The Alamo City has a past; it's one of the oldest cities in the New World, with one of the most popular historical site in Texas—the Alamo. Millions come each year to see the cradle of Texas liberty. The famous courageous trio—Davey Crockett, Colonel William Travis, and James Bowie—are buried in the nearby San Fernando Cathedral. Be sure to see the award-winning IMAX feature **The Alamo, The Price of Freedom** at the Rivercenter Mall.

I loved staying at the Riverwalk Inn. This bed and breakfast, constructed of old log cabins from Tennessee, abounds in charm, with fireplaces in guests' rooms and antique quilts on the beds. After a day of sight-seeing, you're greeted with fresh homemade goodies and lemonade. Believe me, it was tough to leave.

San Antonio is a special place and I can't wait to share this adventure with you. As always, have fun.

Karen Foulk

Table of Contents

Locations

Chapter 1
WHAT'S SAN ANTONIO GOT TO SHOW OFF?

ALAMO

300 Alamo Plaza, San Antonio 78205
210-225-1391

San Antonio's birthplace of Texas liberty

"Remember the Alamo" when you visit San Antonio. Our most sacred historical site is one of the state's top visitor draws. Here, on March 6, 1836, Davy Crockett, Colonel William Travis, Jim Bowie, and 186 other men died defending the Alamo. They fought against Mexican General Santa Ana in a battle that bought Texas freedom.

See what remains of this original mission structure. Visit the chapel and Long Barracks Museum, with mementos of the honored fallen men and artifacts from the Republic of Texas. See the letters these famous men wrote to their families before the battle began.

Tour on your own or arrange to go on a tour. Call to schedule a guide. Either way, you must see the Alamo.

The Alamo, established in 1718 as the Mission San Antonio de Valero, forms part of the greatest concentration of Catholic missions in North America. Successfully extending Spain's dominion from Mexico, these missions converted and educated the Native American Indians. The Alamo is now part of the Missions National Historical Park

Hours
(Closed Christmas Eve and Christmas)

Mon. – Sat. . . . . 9 am – 5:30 pm
Sunday . . . . 10 am – 5:30 pm

Cost - Free

Directions - Located in the heart of downtown. From I-10, exit Houston Street, going toward downtown to Alamo Plaza Street and go right.

8

"Alamo . . . The Price of Freedom"
IMAX THEATER

849 E. Commerce #483
San Antonio 78205
210-225-4629
http://www.imax-sa.com

San Antonio's IMAX features the Alamo

San Antonio's IMAX Theater invites you to see an award-winning feature —"The Alamo . . . The Price of Freedom." With a six-story screen and stereo sound, the IMAX Theater dramatizes the events that took place at the Alamo. Come away with a better understanding and appreciation for what took place. Caution. The feature may be too violent for younger family members. It's realistic, and well done.

Check to see what other interesting shows may be featured. Enjoy a variety of refreshments at the concession stand and visit the unique gift shop with lots of San Antonio memorabilia.

Hours

Daily . . . 9 am, 11 am, 1 pm, 2 pm, 4 pm, 6 pm, 8pm

Cost

Reservation fee $1.50
Adults $7.50
Children 3-11 (free if under 3) $4.75
Seniors 65 . . . . $6.75

Directions

Second level of the Rivercenter Mall, downtown around the corner from the Alamo. Located at Commerce and Bowie Streets.

9

ALAMODOME

100 Montana Street
San Antonio 78203
210-207-3652 or 210-207-3641

San Antonio's new modern stadium

The Alamodome—painted in bright Southwestern colors with a rectangular, cable-suspended roof —adds wonderful flavor to the existing downtown skyline. One of the most experienced firms in the business designed this fantastic stadium.

Home to the San Antonio Spurs, this $186 million state-of-art facility seats 65,000 people and can host professional events such as football, basketball, and ice skating. Among other things, its permanent ice floor meets the U.S. Olympic Committee's requirements. Take the 45-minute guided tour. See what an impressive place this is.

Conveniently located, you can walk from the River Walk, the Alamo, HemisFair Park, and many downtown hotels. Make this part of your sightseeing in San Antonio.

Hours

Group tours with reservations

Tues. – Sat. . . . . 11 am & 1 pm

Cost

Adults $4
Children 4-12 . . . . $2
Children under 4 . . . . Free
Seniors 55+ $2

Directions

Located at I-37 between E. Commerce and
E. Durango Streets.

GHOST STORIES OF HAUNTED PLACES TOURS

Alamo Plaza (in front of the Alamo)
210-436-5417

Go ghost hunting in San Antonio

Tell this to your kids—

"Many believed that the soldiers of the Alamo never received a proper burial. Their souls linger, making San Antonio one of the most haunted cities."

Walk the Alamo City with a "ghost investigator." Tours last 1½ hours. Learn about the most haunted places in San Antonio, where you might have a paranormal experience.

Watch for your guide, a member of the International Ghost Hunters Society. He'll be wearing the black backpack. Make your reservation in advance. Groups of ten or more receive a discount. Call for more details.

Join a special 3-hour "Ghost Hunt" every Saturday night at 10:30 pm. Call for more details. Any teen's idea of fun, right?

Hours

Every night . . . . 8:30 pm

Cost

Adults $10
Children 8 – 17 . . . . $5
Children under 8 . . . . Free

Directions

Meet in front of the Alamo at the defenders' monument, the Cenotaph.

HISTORIC KING WILLIAM DISTRICT WALKING TOUR

A section of town bordering St. Mary's,
Washington, Johnson, and Madison Streets
210-224-6163

San Antonio's classic old homes

Well-to-do German families in the mid-1880s
built elegant Victorian mansions in what was then a
simple frontier town. Today, some of the beautiful old
homes are open to the public only on special
occasions. Still, a walking tour of this unique and
interesting historic district rates high as a favorite
to-do in San Antonio.

Get a copy of the self-guided tour from in front
of the San Antonio Conservation Society Office at
107 King William Street. Wear comfortable shoes and
carry a small jug of ice water when it's hot.

Tour the Steves Homestead, one of the homes
that is open to the public. Top this off with a tasty
lunch at the Guenther House Restaurant. Browse
through the gift shop with delicious baking goods
from Pioneer Mills.

Attend the King William Fair's festive activities
as a part of the Fiesta San Antonio celebration in
April.

Hours

Daily . . . . Until dusk

Cost

Free

Directions

Take St. Mary's Street south of downtown
to King William Street.

MARKET SQUARE

514 W. Commerce, San Antonio 78207
210-207-8600

San Antonio's Mexican Culture

Did you know San Antonio boasts of having the largest Mexican market outside of Mexico? Once a humble farmer's market, it now centers on Mexican culture, with fine restaurants, shops, vendors, mariachi bands, and festivals. Any sightseeing in San Antonio must include Market Square.

One of San Antonio's best restaurants, Mi Tierra opens 24 hours a day. It serves authentic Tex-Mex food made from quality ingredients. Eat here—enjoy tasty breakfasts, lunches, and dinners. See the hand-painted mural on the wall depicting the history of Market Square; stop at the bakery.

The same family that owns Mi Tierra owns and operates La Margarita Mexican Restaurant. This fine restaurant's noisier atmosphere caters to a younger crowd. Open-air patios and strolling mariachis add more pleasure.

Shop at the large indoor center—like those in Mexico. Buy local and imported Mexican goods: jewelry, pottery, Mexican dresses, art, crafts, leather goods, sauces, spices, wrought iron. Newly renovated, the Farmers Market Plaza, once the home of the chili queens, now offers specialty shops and vendors, you won't want to miss. As in Mexico, you can barter for your goods.

Hours

Closed Thanksgiving, Christmas, New Years, and Easter
Summer hours extend until 8 pm

Daily . . . . 10 am – 6 pm

Directions

The market is at Commerce Street and IH-35.

RIVERCENTER MALL

101 Bowie Street
San Antonio 78205
210-225-0000

San Antonio's famous shopping mall

What attracts almost as many tourists as the Alamo? The Rivercenter Mall. This beautiful, well-designed shopping mall with three levels overlooks the River Walk. With over a hundred shops—many unique to San Antonio—you can shop 'til you drop. During the hot summer months, the air-conditioned mall makes a nice diversion from outdoor activities. Plan to spend an evening; the mall remains open after most attractions have closed.

Want a lunch or dinner on the go? Eat at the food court. Vendors at the food court serve excellent food.

Hours

Mon. – Sat. . . . . 10 am – 9 pm
Sunday . . . . Noon – 6 pm

Directions

Located around the corner from the Alamo.
It is on Commerce and Bowie Streets.

RIVER WALK
PASEO DEL RIO

Winds through the downtown area
210-227-4262

One of San Antonio's major attractions

In 1921, the San Antonio River flooded, killing 50 people and destroying millions of dollars in property. Outraged, folks in San Antonio wanted to do away with the river, covering it over with concrete. Fortunately, the women of the San Antonio Conservation Society saved it from this terrible fate.

Now, when people think of San Antonio, they think of the River Walk. The 2.5-mile section of the river stretches from the Henry B. Gonzales Convention Center on the north to the King William Historic District on the south. In between, sidewalk cafes, specialty boutiques, an outdoor theater, a shopping mall, cruises, art galleries, dining on the water, and quiet places to walk attracts thousands.

Don't miss the Fiesta River Parade in April and the Holiday River Parade in December. Annual events include the Mud Festival, when the river is drained for cleaning; St. Patrick's Day, when they dye the river green, and the Christmas Lighting Ceremony, when thousands of lights decorate the river. What a way to capture the holiday spirit.

Hours

Open 24 hours a day.
Cafes and shops open at 10 am.
Most cafes close at 11 pm.

Directions

Enter the River Walk from most downtown streets;
there are over thirty entrances.

SAN ANTONIO CENTRAL LIBRARY

600 Soledad Street
San Antonio 78205
210-207-2500

Visit San Antonio's new library

You can't miss it. Simply look for the bright "red enchilada" building among the downtown buildings. This state-of-the-art library captures everyone's attention and begs for a visit.

Legorreta Arquitectos, a famous architectural firm from Mexico, used bright colors, natural lights, an atrium, and a mystical sense in the designs. As you walk through the library, observe the subtle colors and the different ways light is brought into the building. The atrium extends from the first floor to the sixth floor, with each floor having its own shape and look. Note the courtyard.

The library's highlights include a large genealogical department, a Latino collection, and a wonderful children's library. Children can enjoy puppet shows and story hours.

Hours

Mon. – Thurs.	9 am – 9 pm
Fri. and Sat.	9 am – 5 pm
Sunday	11 am – 5 pm

Directions

Located downtown at Soledad and Navarro Streets.

SAN ANTONIO MISSIONS NATIONAL HISTORIC PARK

2202 Roosevelt Avenue, San Antonio 78210
210-534-8833 or 210-932-1001

A National Historic Park within the city limits

Ever wondered how San Antonio got its start? As early as 1690, Franciscan friars established missions in Texas to convert the Indians to Christianity. Beginning with the Alamo, Mission San Antonio de Valero, five of these missions were built along a 12 mile stretch of the San Antonio River. These fortified communities with churches, housing for the Indians, granaries, mills, farmland and ranchland eventually formed the city of San Antonio—the 8th largest in our country.

You can visit these missions as part of a National Historic Park. Catch a tour. The new $9 million visitor center (at the Mission San Jose, 6701 San Jose Drive, 210-932-1001) features a great video you'll enjoy. It plays every half-hour throughout the day.

Hours:
Open Daily 9 am – 5 pm

Cost: Free

SAN ANTONIO ZOOLOGICAL GARDENS & AQUARIUM

3903 North St. Mary's Street, San Antonio 78212
210-734-7183

San Antonio's zoo rates number one

The zoo, nestled inside an old limestone quarry at the headwaters of the San Antonio River, makes a great family outing. Considered one of our country's finest.

Visit the only zoo with endangered whooping cranes. See rare crocodiles and African Warthogs. And don't miss one of the world's largest lizards with the world's deadliest bite—the Komodo dragons from Indonesia. These lizards can kill animals as large as a water buffalo with a single bite.

Offers an exceptional children's zoo that includes an amphibian exhibit, the Conservation Research Center, a petting zoo, a boat ride, and a playground.

Ask about their season passes—they do save. Concessions are available; enjoy browsing in the gift shops. Wear comfortable shoes and plan to take your time.

Hours

Open every day including holidays
Summer hours extend to 8 pm; gate closes at 6 pm.

Daily . . . . 9 am – 5 pm

Cost

Adults $7
Children 3-11 (under 3 - Free) $5
Seniors 62+ $5

Directions

Go north on North St. Mary's into
Brackenridge Park. Follow the signs.

SAN FERNANDO CATHEDRAL

115 Main Plaza
San Antonio 78205
210-227-1297

San Antonio's famous old cathedral

Visit the oldest cathedral in our country. Named for King Ferdinand III of Spain, who ruled in the 13th century.

At King Phillip V's invitation, fifteen families from the Canary Islands founded the cathedral in 1731 to serve Villa de San Fernando, the original town. The cathedral, after surviving several floods and fires, continues today as a center of religious, community, and cultural events.

James Bowie, one of the important defenders of the Alamo, married here in 1831. See his tomb in the southeast corner of the church. Bowie, Colonel William Travis, and Davy Crockett are buried in the church.

Pope John Paul II visited the cathedral in 1987— a first for Texas. A marble stone marker, inside the church, commemorates the event.

Each year the cathedral performs a Passion Play on Good Friday that reenacts the story of Christ. Attend this special event. Browse in the gift shop with religious items and souvenirs. Opens daily 9:30 am – 4:30 pm.

Hours

Open daily . . . . 9:30 am – 4:30 pm

Cost

Donations are accepted

Directions

The cathedral is on Main Plaza, between Commerce Street and Market Street, in downtown San Antonio.

SEAWORLD SAN ANTONIO

10500 Seaworld Drive
San Antonio 78251
210-523-3611

San Antonio has the biggest marine park

Here, deep in heart of Texas, you'll find the world's largest marine park. The park's abundant of marine life includes, of course, the famous killer whales Shamu and Grandbaby Shamu. Experience penguins, sea lions, walruses, beluga whales, otters, and many more animals up close and in a personal way. Pet the dolphins. Watch many of these animals perform amazing stunts in Seaworld's ever-popular shows that will impress the whole family.

Besides having a marine park, SeaWorld San Antonio offers other attractions, including an inverted roller coaster, a children's play area, a water park, several rides and slides. Plan to get wet and spend the day.

Hours

Seasonal

Cost

Adults $32.95
Children 3-11 . . . . $22.95
Children under 3 . . . . Free
Seniors (55+) get a $3 discount

Directions

Located northwest of San Antonio, between 410 West and Loop 1604 on Highway 151.

SIX FLAGS FIESTA TEXAS

17000 I-10 West
San Antonio 78257
210-697-5050 800-473-4378
www.sixflags.com

San Antonio's new theme park

Want to ride the world's highest and fastest wooden roller coaster? Ride the Rattler, the best of roller coasters or ride the Joker's Revenge a roller coaster that goes in reverse. Other highlights include the Gully Washer, a rapid river ride, and a water park. Bring your swim suit and a towel.

This $100 million theme park features Texas' culture and America's past. Enjoy visiting the German, the Mexican, the Old West, and the 1950's Rock N' Roll sections of the park.

Every evening during the summer see a spectacular laser show with fireworks. Very impressive. Stay for the show.

The park offers plenty of food booths, strollers, pet kennels, lockers, foreign currency exchange, and wheelchairs. It is also handicapped accessible.

Hours - Seasonal.

Cost

Person 48" or taller	$36.62
Person under 48"	$18.31
Seniors 55+	$24.77
Children under 2	Free
Parking	$6

Directions

Six Flags Fiesta Texas is 15 minutes from downtown, at I-10 West and Loop 1604. Take exit 555.

TEXAS ADVENTURE THEATER

307 Alamo Plaza
San Antonio 78205
210-227-8224

Enjoy this fun attraction

With the help of sophisticated technology, the ghost-like images of Davy Crockett, Colonel William Travis, and James Bowie appear and tell their stories in an attraction similar to ones you find at Disney Land.

As you listen to these men, experience the events of the Alamo for yourself. Appreciate the desire of Texans for freedom.

The hour-long presentation entertains and educates. Your family will enjoy going here. They also have a gift shop and snack bar.

Hours

(Show starts every 30 minutes on the hour and half-hour)
Daily .... 10 am – 8 pm

Cost

Adults $7.50
Children 3-11 .... $4.50
Seniors $6

Directions

Located across from the Alamo.

TOWER OF THE AMERICAS

600 HemisFair Park
San Antonio 78205
210-207-8615 Observation deck

Get a good look at San Antonio

The Tower of the Americas, constructed for the World's Fair in 1968, stands 750 feet high and offers a spectacular view of the city on any clear day. Take a ride in a glass elevator to a public observation deck. Enjoy the view a little longer; stay for lunch or dinner in the revolving Tower of the Americas Restaurant, 210-223-2101.

Hours

For observation deck elevators

Sun. – Thurs. . . . . 9 am – 10 pm
Fri. – Sat. . . . . 9 am – 11 pm

Cost

Adults $3
Children 4 -11 . . . . $1
Children under 4 . . . . free
Seniors 55+ $2

Directions

In HemisFair Park, with the entrance at Alamo Street, between Market and Nueva Streets.

WITTE MUSEUM & THE H.E.B. SCIENCE TREEHOUSE

3801 Broadway, San Antonio 78209
210-357-1900

San Antonio's adventure museum

Want to learn and have fun at the same time? Go to the Witte Museum. Its newest addition, the H.E.B. Science Treehouse with hands-on exhibits, makes learning fun. Compose music with laser beams, surf the Internet, launch tennis balls, or lift yourself up with pulleys and ropes. Hear native birds of South Texas or see x-rays and medical test results done on an ancient mummy—don't miss this one. And that's not all. With four levels of activities, plan on staying for hours. Entertaining for all ages.

Besides the H.E.B. Science Treehouse, the museum features a fine collection of Texas paintings, ancient Indian cave paintings, dinosaur fossils from Texas, and displays of our state's different ecological areas.

The Witte Museum sits at the edge of Brackenridge Park. The grounds around the museum include three historic homes and native plants that attract butterflies and hummingbirds. Visit the gift shops.

Hours & Costs

Open until 6 pm in the summer. Closed Thanksgiving, Christmas Eve & Day

Mon., Wed. - Sat.	10 am – 5 pm
Tuesday	10 am – 9 pm
Sunday	Noon - 5 pm
Adults	$5. 95
Children 4–11 (under 4 are free)	$3.95
Seniors 65+	$4.95
Tuesday 3 pm – 9 pm	Free

Directions - North of downtown on Broadway.

YANAGUANA CRUISES

315 E. Commerce
San Antonio 78205
210-244-5700

Cruise the San Antonio River

Yanaguana means "clear or refreshing", the Indian name for the San Antonio River. Enjoy a 40-minute guided narrative cruise along the River Walk. Learn about its history and interesting points. Cruises leave every ½ hour, depending on the season.

Use the water taxi service to go along River Walk. With 9 different stops, conveniently get from major hotels such as the Sheraton, the Adam's Mark, the Marriott and the Landing to where ever you need to go. Rides cost $3.50. For $10, get a day pass, or for $25, a 3-day pass.

Dine aboard one of the cruises. Make reservations for a candlelight dinner cruise with some of the restaurants featured on the River Walk.

Hours

Open holidays

Daily .... 9 am – 10 pm

Cost

for narrative tour

Adults $5.25
Children under 5 .... $1
Seniors $3.65

Directions

Ticket stations: Rivercenter, across from the Hilton Palacio del Rio and the Holiday Inn River Walk.

Locations

1. Bandera Dude & Guest Ranches
2. Blanco State Park
3. Brackenridge Park
4. Canyon Lake
5. Casa Navarro State Historical Park
6. Cascade Caverns
7. Cave-Without-A-Name
8. Cibolo Nature Center and Wildlife
9. Float the Medina River
10. Friederick Wilderness Park
11. Fort Sam Houston Quadrangle
12. Frio Country Cabins and Campsites
13. Garner State Park
14. Guadalupe River State Park
15. HemisFair Park
16. Hill Country State Natural Area
17. Horseback Riding in the San Antonio Area
18. Lost Maples State Natural Area
19. Medina Lake
20. Natural Bridge Caverns
21. Natural Bridge Wildlife Ranch
22. Neal's Lodges
23. Old Tunnel Bat Cave
24. San Antonio Botanical Gardens
25. Sebastopol State Historical Park
26. Union Stockyards of San Antonio

26

Chapter 2
THE GREAT OUTDOORS
Nature, Caves, Parks, Dude Ranches, Zoos

BANDERA DUDE AND GUEST RANCHES

The "Cowboy Capital of the World" in San Antonio's backyard

ABUNDARE RIVER RANCH

HCI, Box 433; Bandera 78003, 830-796-4076

Stay at this 600-acre guest ranch on the Medina River. The ranch offers guests tennis, a pool, a playground, and a gift shop. Sleep in plantation-style accommodations.

Directions - 4 miles southeast of Bandera. Take 173 to Bottle Springs Road and go 2.5 miles.

CHUKKA CREEK GUEST RANCH

Rt. 1, Box 801; Bandera 78003, 830-460-3715

Stay at a ranch that offers trail rides, cattle drives, and cottages with kitchenettes.

Directions - 5 miles west of Bandera on FM 470.

DIXIE DUDE RANCH

P.O. Box 548; Bandera 78003
830-796-4481 • 800-375-9255
www.tourtexas.com/dixieduderanch

Bandera's oldest dude ranch. Guests stay in cabins or in the lodge. The ranch features horseshoes, a heated pool, a playground, basketball and volleyball. Activities include cowboy breakfasts, bonfires, cookouts, hayrides, western entertainment and more. See the old historic barn and cemetery on the premises.

Directions - 9 miles from Bandera on FM 1077.

FLYING L GUEST RANCH

P.O. Box 1959; Bandera 78003
800-292-5134 • 830-460-3001
www.flyingl.com www.flyingl.com

At this ranch, suites come with microwave, refrigerator, and cable TV. Take a trail ride along San Julian Creek or go fishing, hiking, volleyball, and swimming. The ranch has an 18-hole golf course and driving range, also tennis, volleyball, and basketball courts. Children will enjoy the petting corral and playground. Night activities include dancing, campfires, sing-alongs, trick roping, and more. Meals are served buffet style.

Directions - 1 mile from Bandera, South on Hwy 173.

HILL COUNTRY EQUESTRIAN LODGE

1580 Hay Holler Road, Bandera 78003
830-796-7950
www.hillcountryequestlodge.com

Only 10 minutes from Bandera, this 275-acre ranch adjoins the Hill Country State Natural Area, making a 6000-acre horse riding paradise. A bed and breakfast for you and your horse, the facility will board your horse overnight while you stay in a comfy cabin or suite. Or ride one of their horses on a trail ride, (riders must be 6 years old or older). This authentic working ranch is a haven for hikers, bikers, nature lovers, and bird watchers.

Directions - From Bandera, take St. Hwy. 173 S. for ½ miles. Watch for Ranch road 1077 W. Turn right. Go 9.5 miles. At the top of the hill turn right on Hay Holler Road and follow the signs.

LH7 RANCH RESORT

P.O. Box 1474; Bandera 78003 • 830-796-4314

You choose. Accommodations at this ranch include 10 native stone cottages with kitchenettes, 10 RV sites or camping. Activities include hiking, hayrides, nature walks, and bird watching. Be sure to take the ranch tour. See Texas longhorn cattle and enjoy fishing in the lake.

Directions - 5 miles NW of Bandera on FM 3240.

LIGHTNING RANCH

Rt. I, Box 1015; Pipe Creek 78063 • 830-535-4096

The Lightning Ranch's activities include horseback riding, barbecues, hayrides, swimming. Sleep in comfortable cottages.

Directions - .33 miles from Highway 16 on 1283.

MAYAN RANCH

P.O. Box 577; Bandera 78003 • 830-796-3312

With lots to offer, this 324-acre spread runs along the Medina River. You will enjoy swimming, tubing, fishing, hayrides, horseback riding, tennis, pool, and volleyball. Activities also include Texas barbecues, steak cookouts, cowboy breakfasts. For accommodations, stay in one of the cottages or the lodge.

Directions - .5 mi. NW of Bandera on 6th & Pecan.

TWIN ELM GUEST RANCH

P.O. Box 117; Bandera 78003
888-567-3049 • 830-796-3628

Take your choice. This ranch accommodates guests with cabins or bunkhouses. Guests enjoy horseback riding, rodeos, hiking, river swimming, hayrides, fossil hunting, and other fun activities.

Directions - 3 miles NW of Bandera on FM 470.

RUNNING R RANCH

Rt. 1, Box 590; Bandera 78003

830-796-3984

www.rrranch.com

Want to go on a picnic? Guests can request a tasty picnic lunch. The cabin accommodations include 3 meals and horseback riding.

Directions - 9 miles west of Bandera on RR 1077, next to the Hill Country State Natural Area.

SILVER SPUR DUDE RANCH

P.O. Box 1657; Bandera 78003

830-796-3037

www.texasusa.com/ranches/silvspur.html

This ranch's ideal location makes it attractive. Bordering the Hill Country State Natural Area, it offers scenic horseback rides and guest accommodations with home-style cooking. Eat cowboy breakfasts and Texas barbecues. Facilities includes a pool table, a game room, swimming pool, and a playground.

Directions - 10 miles south of Bandera on FM 1077.

THE FARM COUNTRY CLUB

P.O. Box 831; Bandera 78003

830-589-2276

Need a group outing? This ranch caters to group excursions with plenty of activities: barbecues, western bands, trick ropers, hayrides, gunfighters, rodeos, horseshoe pitching, swimming, and more.

Directions - 8 miles from Bandera on FM 2828.

BLANCO STATE PARK

P.O. Box 493
Blanco 78606
830-833-4333
512-389-8900 for reservations

Hill Country camping

Camp where early explorers and settlers camped. Besides camping, the 100-acre park offers swimming, picnicking, hiking, wildlife observing, boating, and fishing. You will enjoy fishing for perch, catfish, bass, and winter rainbow trout. Be sure to hike the beautiful ¾-mile trail. Self-guided maps of the trail are available at the park store. Ask about the guided hiking tour.

The park provides restrooms with showers, campsites with water and electricity, and day-use facilities.

Hours

Daily . . . . 8 am - 10 pm

Cost

Day use fee for adults (13 and older) $3
Campsites . . . . $12 - 14

Directions

Located in Blanco, 40 miles north of San Antonio. Take U.S. Highway 281 to Park Road 23, four blocks south of the town.

The Great **Outdoors**

BRACKENRIDGE PARK

3910 N. St. Mary's Street
San Antonio 78212
210-736-9534

Spend a day at Brackenridge Park

Brackenridge Park's wonderful attractions make it one of the most desirable year-round family destinations in San Antonio. Entertain your family with an endless number of things to do. Featuring one of the ten top zoos in the U.S., this 400-acre scenic park doesn't stop here. Be sure to see the ever-popular Witte Museum with its H.E.B Science Treehouse, the newly renovated Japanese Tea Garden. and the scenic train ride through the trees on the Brackenridge Eagle Miniature Train. The kids will find the Kiddie Park lots of fun.

Each of these attractions has its own operating schedule and admission fee except for the Japanese Tea Garden, which is free.

The family will love having cookouts along the river. The park also has a public golf course and driving range.

Hours (for attractions)

Mon. – Fri. . . . . 9:30 am – 5 pm
Sat. – Sun . . . . 9:30 am – 5:30 pm

Cost
Prices vary with the attraction

Directions

Located 2 miles north of downtown San Antonio. The main entrance is at the 2800 block of Broadway.

CANYON LAKE

U.S. Army Corps of Engineers, Fort Worth Division
HC4, Box 400, New Braunfels 78133-4112
830-964-3341 or 830-964-2223
www.canyonlakechamber.com

One of the most scenic lakes in Texas

Situated in steep hills, Canyon Lake's average depth of 43 feet offers excellent opportunities for water sports, birding, picnicking, camping, and hiking. The Upper Guadalupe River makes available some of best white water kayaking and canoeing in Texas. Below the dam, the river's mild current is a haven for tubers.

Spend the day at one of Canyon Lake's many parks. Located along the shoreline, these parks feature a variety of facilities for day users and campers: Comal Park, Canyon Park, Potter's Creek Park, Overlook Park, Crane's Mill Park, Jacob's Park, and North Park. Some of these parks provide extras such as boat ramps, marines, and convenience stores.

Hours

Day use parks
Summer hours extend until 9 pm

Daily . . . . 7 am – 10 pm

Camping parks (summer only, except for RVs)

Daily . . . . 7 am – 10 pm

Cost

Day use parks

Adults $1
Max. Per car $3
Camping . . . . $6 - $16

Directions

Canyon Lake is 20 miles north of New Braunfels.
Take S. H. 46 and FM 2722 north, or 306 north of I-35.

CASA NAVARRO
STATE HISTORICAL PARK

228 S. Laredo Street
San Antonio
210-226-4801

An interesting historical site

Don Jose Antonio Navarro, born in 1795, contributed much to the state of Texas. He not only ranched, but as a popular statesman, he signed The Texas' Declaration of Independence. He also participated in the convention that brought Texas into the Union. He attended as the only native Texan.

Thanks to the San Antonio Conservation Society, you'll enjoy touring his home. Built in 1848, the house gives visitors a good example of early Texas architecture and furnishings. Exhibits inside the home make early Texas history interesting.

Plan to take the personalized guided tour and take your time.

Hours

Closed Mondays and Tuesdays
Wed. – Sun. 10 am – 4 pm

Cost

Adults $2
Children 6 – 12 . . . . $1
Children under 6 . . . . Free

Directions

In downtown San Antonio on the corner of South Laredo and West Nueva Streets. Use West Nueva.

The Great Outdoors

CASCADE CAVERNS

Cascade Cavern Road, Boerne 78015
830-755-8080

Oldest operating cave in Texas

These caverns date back millions of years. Over time single droplets of water have created what we see today—magnificent formations. See evidence of Indians using the upper caverns for ceremonies and hear stories of an old German hermit who lived in its entrance. Designated as a historical site, the caverns will excite any family looking for a good time.

As you descend 190 feet below the surface, you will see beautiful living formations. Best of all, the tour ends with a grand finale—a 100-foot waterfall. Tours take about 45 minutes. Rubber-soled shoes are a must. The cave is not accessible to strollers and wheelchairs. Bring your camera.

Enjoy the picnic area with barbecue pits and a 105-acre RV park with a swimming pool.

Hours

Summer

Mon.-Fri.	9 am – 6 pm
Sat.-Sun.	10 am – 4 pm

Winter

Mon. – Fri.!	10 am – 5 pm
Sat. – Sun.	9 am – 5 pm

Cost

Adults	$9.50
Children ages 3-11	$5.50
Children under 2	$1

Directions

Take I-10 West from San Antonio 16 miles.
Exit Cascade Caverns Road and follow the signs.

CAVE-WITHOUT-A-NAME

325 Kreutzberg Road, Boerne 78006
830-537-4212

One of the most beautiful caverns in Texas

What would you call these caverns? Over 60 years ago, a contest to name the cave was held. A young boy wrote that he thought it was too pretty to name. Out of hundreds of entries, the owner liked his best. In the '70s, attempts were again made to rename the cave, but the name remains the same today.

Visit one of the largest caves in Texas. See huge underground rooms with beautiful live limestone formations that continue to grow. Rubber-shoed shoes are a must as you wander along the gravel paths and down the concrete stairs that take you over 100 feet below the surface. The tour lasts approximately 1 hour and 15 minutes. Cameras are allowed. It is privately owned and not as well known as other Hill Country caverns. Call ahead before going.

Hours

(Closed weekdays, Christmas & Thanksgiving during the winter)
Six days a week (Closed Tues.). . 9 am – 6 pm

Cost

Adults $8
Children 5 – 11 . . . . $4
Children under 5 . . . . Free

Directions

Located 40 miles northwest of San Antonio. Take I-10 west and exit Hwy 87 which becomes Main Street and follow into Boerne. Continue thru Boerne to the 4th light. Turn right onto 474 and go 6 miles to Kreutzberg Road. Follow signs 5.5 miles to the cave.

CIBOLO NATURE CENTER AND WILDERNESS TRAILS

140 City Park Road, Boerne 78006
830-249-4616

Lunch under giant cypress trees along Cibolo Creek

The four ½-mile nature trails take hikers through woodlands, marshes, and prairie lands, depending on the trail you choose. The Marsh Trail goes across a boardwalk to an observation area. The Woodland Trail is best for warm weather hikes because most of the trail is shaded. This trail leads to the creek where many like to picnic. The scenic creek bed is lined with giant cypress trees. Here you'll find tables and barbecue grills. Then again, if hiking isn't of interest, simply drive down to the creek for a picnic.

The fun Creek Trail winds along the creek. Or you can experience the Prairie Trail that wanders through landscapes of native grasses.

In the Nature Center, kids find the hands-on exhibits fascinating. It's best to call before going. Volunteers run the center and when no one is available, the center remains closed.

At the pavilion, you will find a display of dinosaur tracks that were discovered at the Boerne Lake Spillway during the June 1997 flood. The center offers summer concerts, be sure to ask about this. If bird watching is of interest, put this place on your to-do list.

Hours (Trails)

Daily . . . . 8:30 am – 10 pm

Cost (donations appreciated) - Free

Directions

From San Antonio, take I-10 N to the Boerne exit, Hwy. 87. Travel through town. Turn right on River Rd, Hwy. 46, and go 3/4 mile. Turn right on City Park Rd. Watch for signs

FLOAT THE MEDINA RIVER

Float through scenic Hill Country on the Medina River—from Medina to Bandera. The following outfits rent tubes, canoes, and/or kayaks and will help you pick a put-in and take-out spot. The Medina River is great for families. The river is ideal for beginner kayakers and canoers. Rapids are usually entertaining, not intimidating. Call for more information.

Fred Collins Workshop
Highway 16 North, Bandera 78003
830-796-3553
Rents tubes for $5 and kayaks for $25 a day. Shuttles rides are extra. The shop opens daily at 8 am.

Rev's Bandera Beach Club & Tube Rental
Highway 16 North, Bandera 78003
888-660-3950 or 796-7555
Tube rentals for $5 a day and $2 for a shuttle ride.

Yogi Bear's Jellystone Park
Highway 173 South, Bandera 78003
830-796-3751
Rents tubes and canoes.

Medina Kayaks & River Ranch
Highway 16 North, Medina
830-589-7215
Rents kayaks. This outfitter rents different kinds: sit-on-top kayaks, sit-inside kayaks, and even double-seat kayaks. Prices range $15-$40/day. Group rates are available. Use the kayaks to float any where you like.

FORT SAM HOUSTON QUADRANGLE

Building 123 S4 Road, Ft. Sam Houston
San Antonio 78234
210-221-1151

Fort Sam Houston is rich in history

Fort Sam Houston's rich history dates back to 1845, when Texas joined the Union and the U.S. Army moved to Texas. After building a permanent fort in 1870, the army constructed the quadrangle, with its famous brick clock tower, as a supply depot.

Popular with folks, the fort makes the quadrangle available to the public. The quadrangle houses many tame animals: white-tailed deer, chickens, rabbits, squirrels, geese, ducks, and peafowl. According to legend, these animals descended from those brought here by Geronimo. He lived in the quadrangle for a while as prisoner with other Apache warriors.

In 1898, Theodore Roosevelt's Rough Riders stopped at the quadrangle for supplies on their way to Cuba. They camped in an area now known as Roosevelt Park.

Today the headquarters for the 5th U.S. Army resides at Fort Sam Houston. While on base, enjoy these two museums: the Ft. Sam Houston Museum and the U.S. Army Medical Museum.

Hours

Mon. – Fri. . . . . 8 am – 6 pm
Sat. and Sun. . . . . Noon – 5 pm

Cost - Free

Directions

At Fort Sam Houston, the corner of Grayson St. and New Braunfels Ave. Take Broadway north to Grayson St. and go right.

FRIEDRICH WILDERNESS PARK

21480 Milsa, San Antonio 78256
210-698-1057 Park Naturalist

A popular place for enjoying the great outdoors & guided interpretive hikes

Get out the hiking boots. Friedrich Wilderness Park provides an easy escape from the hectic urban life of San Antonio. Located in forested hills, the park makes available opportunities for hiking, picnicking, and birding.

Hikers get a choice in hiking trails. Take an easy one like the Upland Range Trail or experience more of a challenge on trails like the Vista Loop and the Main Loop Trails. All trails are well marked with map boards. Folks in wheelchairs will enjoy the Forest Ranger Trail. Arrange for a guided interpretive hike with a park naturalist. Call for details.

You'll find an abundance of wildlife: white-tailed deer, cottontail rabbits, squirrels, and raccoons. As a favorite spot for birding, the park offers a chance to see rare species of birds like the golden-cheeked warbler and the black-capped vireo. Other birds such as the northern orioles, painted bunting, northern bobwhites, and greater roadrunners frequent the area.

Depending on the weather and time of year, the park tends to be crowded. Beat the crowds on weekdays or during the summer and winter months.

April-September *(Tues. – Sun. only)*   8 am – 8 pm
October-March *(Tues. – Sun. only)*   8 am – 5 pm

Cost - Free

Directions - In northwest San Antonio. Take I-10 West to the Camp Bullis Road Exit. Turn left and go on the underpass, then right on the access road. Go 1 mile and turn left on Oak Drive. Follow to a T intersection and go right on Milsa.

FRIO COUNTRY CABINS AND CAMPSITES

P.O. Box 188
Concan 78838
830-232-6625

Exciting family retreat

A great place if you want to get away for a weekend. You'll find 60 air-conditioned cabins plus campsites located on the cool, clear Frio River. Inner tubing at its finest. Most who stay here make reservations to return before leaving.

Offers a country store with picnic supplies. Float trips are available. Over 30 campsites with electricity and water, 10 campsites for tent camping.

Seasonal

Open from May through September. July is the peak season. Frio Country takes reservations anytime.
During the peak season, a three-night stay is required.

Cost

Cabin prices are based on four people;
prices start at $100 a night.

Directions

Located approximately 80 miles west of San Antonio on the Frio River. From San Antonio, take Highway 90 west to Sabinal. Turn right on Highway 127/187 at the only red light. Go through the city of Sabinal (in about 2 miles the highway separates). Take Highway 127, about 20 miles. Just before Highway 127 ends and hits Highway 83, turn right on River Road. Frio Country Store and office is 2 miles on River Road, on the left.

GARNER STATE PARK

HCR #70 Box 599, Concan 78838
830-232-6132 • 512-389-8900 for reservations

The most visited park in Texas

Named after John Nance Garner, a former U.S. Vice President, Garner State Park opened in 1941. The park developed and improved with the help of the Civilian Conservation Corp.

Situated in the beautiful Hill Country. The clear, rock-bottomed Frio River flows through the park, creating all kinds of recreational opportunities and attracting lots of guests for many reasons. The park features camping, hiking, nature study, picnicking, boating, fishing, swimming, and biking. And during the summer, enjoy dancing every evening, playing miniature golf, and tubing on the river.

The park's campsites provide water; some also have electricity. Rent paddleboats and inner tubes. The park facilities also include screened shelters, picnic tables, and a dining hall. Stay in one of the 17 CCC-built cabins.

Office hours

Daily . . . . 8 am – 5 pm

Cost

Entrance fee (overnight campers) 13+ $3
Entrance fee (day use per person) 13+ . . . $5
Campsites w/water . . . . $10 -$15
Campsites w/water and electricity . . $15 -$20
Shelters . . . . $20 -$25
Cabins . . . . $70 -$75

Directions

Eight miles north of Concan on the Frio River. Take U.S. Hwy 83, turn east on FM 1050 and go .5 mile to Park Rd 29, follow to the entrance.

GUADALUPE RIVER RANCH

605 FM 474, Boerne 78006
800-460-2005 Reservations
830-537-4837

Swing in a hammock; admire the Hill Country view

Here's a great getaway for families wanting to relax and enjoy life. Situated on the banks of the Guadalupe River, this ranch's list of things to do is endless: horseback riding, hiking, kayaking, canoeing, tubing, mountain biking, tennis, swimming, and bird watching. Enjoy plenty of yard games like volleyball and horseshoes.

Amenities include two pools, a sauna, hot tub, and an exercise room. Or you can simply swing in the hammock or on the porch swing, enjoy the view while reading a book.

Stay in screened-in porch cottages or the two-story condos with terrific views that sleep up to four people.

Trail rides take place every morning at 9:30 am. Children under 6 will enjoy corral rides—horse riding geared just for them.

Your stay at the ranch includes breakfast and dinner. Additional family members cost extra. Lunch and activities are extra too. Weekend stays require reservations for two nights; holidays, for three nights. Popular thing to do. Make reservations well in advance.

Hours (Office)

Daily . . . . 7 am – 11 pm

Cost (includes breakfast & dinner)

Per night (for two) $239

Directions

Take I-10 West out of San Antonio. Travel 22 miles to Boerne, then exit #542. Turn right at the town square onto Hwy. 474. Go 8 miles to the ranch.

GUADALUPE RIVER STATE PARK

3350 Park Road 31
Spring Branch 78070
830-438-2656
512-389-8900 for reservations

Enjoy tubing the Guadalupe River

Make your reservations well in advance. The 1938-acre park tends to be busy in the summertime and on holidays. People love to go tubing on the Guadalupe River and the park provides an ideal place to camp along the river. You'll also enjoy the rugged beauty of this scenic park.

Other activities include fishing, swimming, canoeing, picnicking, wildlife observing, and hiking. See armadillos, white-tailed deer, squirrels, raccoons, and a variety of birds.

Hours

Open year round

Daily .... 8 am – 10 pm

Cost

Day use per person 13+ $4
Camping $12-15

Directions

Located 30 miles north of San Antonio. Go 8 miles west of junction U.S. Highway 281 and U.S. Highway 46 to Park Road 31, then 3 miles to the entrance.

HEMISFAIR PARK

200 South Alamo
San Antonio 78205

Visit the park with the tower

San Antonio celebrated its 200th birthday with the 1968 World's Fair. The site of the World's Fair, HemisFair Park, still hosts attractions you'll want to include in your sightseeing trips.

See The Water Park's 12 acres of fountains, wading pools, and landscaping that make the park a pleasant place to stroll. Be sure to take the elevators to the observation deck of the Tower of the Americas and lunch in the revolving restaurant.

The Downtown All-Around Playground built by volunteers will entertain any child for hours. The playground features a wood-constructed play area with a space tunnel and castle.

Best of all visit the Institute of Texan Cultures, a museum about the different cultural influences in San Antonio and South Texas.

Hours

Open 24 hours a day

Directions

The entrance is on Alamo Street between Market and Nueva Streets.

HILL COUNTRY STATE NATURAL AREA

Route 1, Box 601, FM 1077, Bandera 78003
830-796-4413 • 512-389-8900 for reservations

Scenic trails for hiking and riding

The only state park that allows horseback riding. This rugged 5000-acre park features miles of trails for horseback riding, hiking, mountain biking, primitive camping, and backpacking. Numerous ranches in the area provide horses and trail rides. Trails for riding or hiking range from easy to difficult. Some have wonderful scenic views and rock canyons up to 1,900 feet in elevation.

Swim in the spring-fed creek or plan to go fishing. Sections of the area are available for off-road cyclists. You'll delight in the wildlife: white-tailed deer, lizards, red-tailed hawks, and more.

The park offers no amenities such as potable water, paved roads, or restrooms. Plan to bring your own supplies. Overnight camping is not allowed on Monday nights. Call the information hotline, 800-792-1112, before going, especially during hunting season.

Hours

Spring, Summer and Fall - Open 24 hours a day
Winter - Camping and hiking is allowed from
noon on Fridays until 10 pm on Sundays

Cost

Day use fee (over 13) . . . . $3 each
Day use fee (under 13) . . . . $2 each

Directions

45 miles NW of San Antonio. Hwy 16 to Bandera. South on Hwy 173 one mile, then FM 1077 for 10 mi.

HORSEBACK RIDING IN THE SAN ANTONIO AREA

Here are ways to enjoy horseback riding

Rent a horse from the following outfits. Horses rent by the hour. Some offer half-day and full-day rides and will include meals. Contact the following for more details.

CHUKKA CREEK

830-460-3715

Half- and full-day rides. Mornings include breakfast. See Texas Longhorn cattle and an abundant of wildlife.

DESERT HEARTS COWGIRL CLUB

830-796-7446

Features 2-hour rides in the Hill Country.

HILL COUNTRY EQUESTRAIN LODGE

830-796-7950

Private instruction and personalized trail rides for up to 3 people. Ride in beautiful Hill Country State Natural Area. Must be 6 years old or older

LOMA DE BLANCA

830-741-4596

Horseback riding, camping, and lodging with meals.

LH7 LONGHORN OUTFITTERS

830-796-4314

Scenic rides. Longhorn cattle.

LIGHTNING RANCH
830-535-4096 • 830-668-4096
Horseback riding for 2 hr, half-day, or full-day. Lunch and camping equipment furnished.

LIGHTNING'S HORSEBACK TOURS
830-460-8182
Customized rides. Offers 1 hour, 2 hour, 1/2 day, all day, and overnight rides.

RUNNING R RANCH
830-796-3984
Scenic rides on ranch with guides.
Must be at least 6 years old.

SILVER SPUR DUDE RANCH
830-796-3037
Horseback riding on scenic ranch.

TWIN ELM GUEST RANCH
830-796-3628
Morning rides on hilltop with view; afternoon rides along the river.

WAGON WHEEL STABLES
830-966-2153
Offers guided trail rides. All riders welcome.

LOST MAPLES STATE NATURAL AREA

HCO1 Box 156, Vanderpool 78885
830-966-3413

Experience the Hill Country 1st hand

Hike deep in the heart of the Texas Hill Country. This wilderness preserve offers two scenic 5-mile hiking loops—a must do. Over a 100,000 people hike these trails in the park's most popular months—October and November.

Hikers must obtain a permit from the headquarters. The hiking can be strenuous at times. Come prepared with all the backpacking essentials and plenty of drinking water.

The park offers day-use facilities and 30 campsites with electricity and water. If you like, purchase a souvenir tee shirt at the park's headquarters.

Although the park's office closes earlier, guests using the day-use facilities may stay until 10 pm.

Hours

Mon. – Thurs.	8 am – 5 pm
Fri. – Sun.	8 am – 8 pm

Cost *(Park entrance and day use fee)*

Adults 13+	$4

(Except in Oct. & Nov. fees are $5 for adults)

Children under 13	Free

Camping

Per night	$14 + $2 entrance fee/per
Backpacking	$8 + $2 entrance fee/per

Directions

From San Antonio take Hwy 16 to Medina. Outside Medina turn left on Hwy 337. Follow Hwy 337 until it deadends at Hwy 187. Go right 4 miles to the park.

LOVE CREEK ORCHARD'S PICK-YOUR-OWN PARK

944 FM 2200 West
Devine 78016
800-449-0882 or 830-589-2588

Pick peachy peaches on a fun family outing

Before going to this Pick-Your-Own farm, call for a "ripe report" or for picking availability. These peaches taste juicy and sweet—the Florida Crest variety. You pick them by the container May through June. The farm also offers blackberries about the same time.

Containers come in different sizes. And the more you pick, the more it's a bargain.

Remember to wear comfortable, cool clothing, bring sunscreen and bug spray, and a jug of ice water. Families welcome.

Hours
(During the picking season)
Daily . . . . 8:30 am – 7 PM

Cost
5 pound container $5
10 pound container $10
25 pound container $24

Directions
Take I-35 South to Devine. Exit Hwy. 173. Go right on Hwy. 173 and continue through 3 stoplights. Turn left on FM 2200. Go 1.3 miles. The farm is on the right.

MEDINA LAKE
Scenic lake in the Hill Country

The 5575-acre Medina Lake situated in the hills and limestone bluffs provides excellent fishing for yellow catfish. Plan to spend the day catching varieties of bass, catfish, crappie, and shad. You will enjoy the lake's amenities: camping, boating, picnicking, and water sports. Medina Lake is a favorite for divers.

Pubskis Water Sports (830-612-2038) located at Park Road 37 at 34th Street in Lake Hills, TX. offers rentals on Pontoon, fishing, and ski boats. They also rent jet skis and provide a fishing guide service.

Hours
Daily . . . . Dawn to dusk

Cost
Call for rental fees

Directions
Located 30 miles west San Antonio on FM 1283. Enter the park on Park Road 37.

NATURAL BRIDGE CAVERNS

26495 Natural Bridge Caverns Road
Natural Bridge Caverns 78266
210-651-6101
www.naturalbridgetexas.com\caverns

Visit the largest underground caverns in Texas

Water still drips from the ceiling of the old caverns as the massive, colorful formations continue to grow. Hear underground water gushing overhead. See underground rooms the size of football fields.

In 1960, ranchers allowed four college students to explore the cave. Surprised, the men discovered a 60-foot passageway that lead to huge underground cavern systems. The caverns were opened to the public in 1964.

You'll find the guided narrative tour fascinating. Wear cool comfortable clothing. The caverns remain at 70 degrees year-round, but with humidity over 90%, the temperature feels much warmer. The tour takes 1 hours and 15 minutes. Athletic shoes or shoes with rubber soles are a must. Strollers are allowed, but there are two narrow stairways.

Hours

Summer hours extend to 6 pm

Daily . . . . 9 am – 4 pm

Cost

Adults $12
Children 4 – 12 . . . . $7
Children under 4 . . . . Free
Seniors 65+ $10

Directions

From San Antonio, take IH 35 north to exit #175 (Natural Bridge Caverns Road) 3009 and go east 8 miles.

The Great *Outdoors*

NATURAL BRIDGE WILDLIFE RANCH

26515 Natural Bridge Caverns Road
Natural Bridges Caverns 78266
830-438-7400
www.nbwildliferanchtx.com

See exotic animals from your car

Your admission fee will include a bag of feed for the animals. (And the animals know that.) That's what's fun about the Natural Bridge Wildlife Ranch. Be prepared as you drive into the park; eager animals will swarm your car in anticipation of a handout. It's the ostriches and the llamas, however, that provide the greatest thrill. If you survive, stop in at the gift shop for your "I survived the ostriches" tee shirt.

The wildlife park features animals from all over the world. Animals roam the open ranchland, allowing visitors to view them in a natural setting.

Take the kids to the petting zoo and to see the other caged animals. Be sure to visit the gift shop for souvenirs of your adventure. Your kids will be love this one.

Hours

Daily (til 6:30 pm - Summer) .... 9 am – 5 pm

Cost

Adults $9.50
Children 3-11 .... $6
Children under 3 .... Free
Seniors 65+ $8

Directions

From San Antonio, take IH 35 north to exit #175 (Natural Bridge Caverns Road) 3009 and go east 8 miles.

NEAL'S LODGES

P.O. Box 165 (Hwy 127)
Concan 78838
830-232-6118

A favorite family vacation spot

One of the best-kept secrets in Texas. Located on the beautiful Frio River in the heart of the Hill Country. Rent one of their 66 cabins. Choose from rustic cabins that are favorites of many to ones that are more lavish.

Offers RV hookups, camping facilities near the river, a country store, a restaurant, a washateria, a video game room, hayrides, horseback riding, innertube rentals, and much more.

Reservations are taken as early as January 1 for the entire year. A deposit and a three-night stay are required in the summer.

Summer Season

Memorial Day through Labor Day

Cost

Cabins per night	$55 - $190
Per person hayrides	$6
Horse rides	$15/hr.
Float trips	$2
Innertubes	$4
Campsites	$19.50
RV Hookups	$25

Directions

Located 80 miles west of San Antonio in the town of Concan, go 23 miles north of Uvalde on Highway 127.

OLD TUNNEL BAT CAVE
830-644-2478
Watch a bat show

See millions of bats fly out in a whirlwind—something like a tornado—from an old abandoned railroad tunnel—every evening from March through October. Definitely a fun thing to do.

The old railroad tunnel was built in the early 1900s. The Frederickburg and Northern Railway Company abandoned the tunnel in 1942. Since then the old tunnel has become a seasonal home for millions of Mexican Free-Tail bats.

Bats emerge from the tunnel between 8:05 pm and 8:20 pm and head southeast in search of insects. Visitors are welcome to view this fascinating phenomenon from the parking lot. Better yet, on Thursdays and Saturdays, a park ranger gives a very informative talk at 7 pm. Learn about the bats, the tunnel and the area. Seating for the talk is limited to 60 people, so plan to arrive early. The Texas Parks and Wildlife now preserves and protects this area.

Guided Tour Hours
March - October

Thurs. & Sat.	7 pm

Guided Ranger Cost
Park and view on your own for free

Adults	$5
Children 17 & under	$2
Children under 5	Free
Seniors	$3

Directions
Take I-10 to Comfort, exit Hwy 87. Head towards Comfort. Turn left on Hwy 473—outside of Comfort. When Hwy 473 turns right towards Sisterdale, keep going straight on Old No. 9 Road. Travel to Alamo Road. The tunnel is on the right. Watch for sign.

SAN ANTONIO BOTANICAL GARDENS

555 Funston Place, San Antonio 78209
210-207-3250

Considered one of the finest

Lush describes the gardens. Whether you like roses or wildflowers, you'll delight in what you'll see here. The botanical gardens portray many different native Texas landscapes and other interesting vistas. The Biblical Garden shows off plants referred to in the Bible such as fig trees and date palms. The blind will enjoy the Touch and Scent Garden—everyone else will, too. With interpretive signs in Braille, the garden yields plants interesting to our other senses. And for the kids visit the especially designed Children's Garden.

The award-winning, $6.5 million Lucile Halsell Conservatory Complex contains 90,000 square feet of climate-controlled space. Explore the tropical house, the desert house, the palm house, the fern house, and much more.

The San Antonio Conservation Society's efforts preserved the 1896 Carriage House that now houses the gift shop and tearoom.

Hours
Closed Christmas & New Year's
(Nov.–Feb.) Daily . . . . 8 am – 5 pm
(Mar.–Oct.) Daily . . . . 9 am – 6 pm

Cost
Adults $4
Children 3-13 (under 3 Free) $1
Senior 55+ $2

Directions
Five minutes from downtown. Take Broadway north to Funston and go right. Entrance will be on the left.

SEBASTOPOL STATE HISTORICAL PARK

704 Zorn Street, Sequin 78155
830-379-4833

See this unique old house

In a vista of 300-year-old live oaks and antique roses, this old pioneer home, built in 1856, is one of the finest examples of early Greek Revival architecture. The State of Texas recognizes the house as a Registered Texas Historic Landmark and it lists with the National Register of Places.

The limecrete construction gives the house special notice. Only a few such houses with this unusual and unique construction still remain. Let your personal tour guide explain how they were built.

See the original furnishings on the upper level of the home. You'll find it interesting to learn about the Zorn family — who owned and maintained the home for generations. As a turn-of-the-century mayor, Joseph Zorn loved innovations. His progressive thinking resulted in a power plant on the Guadalupe River, which brought electricity to the small town of Sequin.

Hours

Fri. – Sun. . . . . . . 9 am – Noon & 1 pm – 4 pm

Cost

Adults $2
Students 6–12 . . . . $1
Children under 5 . . . . $.50

Directions

30 minutes from San Antonio. Take I-10 to S.H. 46 south one mile and turn left onto Court Street. The park will be one mile on your left.

UNION STOCKYARDS OF SAN ANTONIO

1716 S. San Marcos Street
San Antonio 78207
210-223-6331

Visit these famous old stockyards

In early frontier days, farmers marketed their agricultural goods in San Antonio. After the Civil War, cattle drivers on their way to northern markets stopped here for their supplies.

With the arrival of the railroad, the cattle business changed. Ranchers then sold their cattle to buyers who shipped them to markets by rail. In 1889 a group of ranchers formed the San Antonio Stockyards Company to meet the demands of the cattle industry. Today, these 100-year-old stockyards continue as a major trading center for livestock.

You'll get a thrill watching real working cowboys at the oldest stockyard west of the Mississippi. Public auctions continue every Monday and Wednesday morning. Visitors are welcome.

Hours

Mondays and Wednesdays . . . . Begins at 9 am

Cost

Free

Directions

From I-10, take S.H. 35 North, exit San Marcos and follow to the stockyards.

Locations

1. Air Force History and Traditions Museum
2. Buckhorn Saloon and Museum
3. Espada Aqueduct and Acequia
4. Fort Sam Houston Museum
5. Hanger 9 / Edward H. White Museum
6. Hertzberg Circus Museum
7. Institute of Texans Cultures
8. La Villita Historic District
9. Mexican Cultural Institute
10. McNay Art Museum
11. Pioneer Trail Drivers and Texas Ranger Memorial Museum
12. San Antonio's Children's Museum
13. San Antonio Museum of Art
14. Spanish Governor's House
15. Steves Homestead
16. Texas Transportation Museum
17. U.S. Army Medical Museum
18. Yturri-Edmunds Museum

DOWNTOWN SAN ANTONIO

Chapter 3
SAN ANTONIO'S MUSEUMS AND HISTORY

AIR FORCE HISTORY AND TRADITIONS MUSEUM

Building 5206
Lackland Air Force Base
210-671-3055

See a military aviation museum

Focusing on our military aviation history, the museum's collection includes rare aircraft and aircraft components from World War I to the present. See engines, weapons, and memorabilia housed inside the museum and a static display of aircraft outside on base grounds. The display of aircraft features World War II, Vietnam, and other aircraft, including an SR-71 Blackbird.

Enjoy the variety of military aviation videos the museum's theater has to offer. The museum also has a library.

Hours

Closed federal holidays
Mon. – Fri. . . . . 8 am – 4:30 pm

Cost

Free

Directions

From Military Drive to the Luke entrance.
Go left on Jary and follow it around to Orville Wright Drive. Take a right. Building 5206 will be straight ahead.

BUCKHORN SALOON AND MUSEUM

318 E. Houston Street, San Antonio 78205
210-247-4000

See rare and exotic collections of wildlife

In 1881, trappers and cowboys exchanged deer antlers for a drink in Albert Friedrich's saloon. Numerous antlers now hang on the saloon's walls. Today, the collections also include the Hall of Horns, the Hall of Feathers, and the Hall of Fins—taxidermy examples of exotic and native wildlife—with numerous dioramas and exhibits. The Hall of Horns is considered to be the world's largest collection of antlers.

The museum affords visitors the opportunities to see animals that are rare or extinct like, Passenger Pigeons and the Irish elk antlers. The wax museum, the Hall of Texas History features life-size figures of heroes and other influential people from 1532 – 1898.

Enjoy seeing the Lone Star Buckhorn Museum at its new downtown location. Take a guided tour or tour on your own. Tour ends with a complimentary beer or root beer.

Hours

Daily . . . . 10 am – 6 pm

Cost

Adults $7.99
Children (4 - 11) $5.50
Children under 4 . . . . Free
Seniors $7.00

Directions

Downtown at Houston and Navarro Streets.

ESPADA ACEQUIA AND AQUEDUCT

9044 Espada
210-534-8833 Missions National Historic park
www.nps.gov/saan/

See a 250-year-old irrigation system

In the 1700's, Spanish missionaries and Indians constructed five dams, seven gravity-flow ditches, and an aqueduct—a 15-mile network of irrigation ditches—to carry water to their fields. The watering system resembles ones found in Spain, built by the Moslems. The system supplied water for almost 3500 acres of farmland.

Many of the canals no longer exist. Examples of the acequia can be found around San Antonio: at the Alamo, in HemisFair Park, and at the Yturri-Edmunds Historic Site.

Take a drive south of downtown on the Mission Trail to the Espada Dam. See where the water empties into the acequia madre—the mother of all ditches—and then the Espada Aqueduct, one of the oldest arched Spanish aqueducts in the United States. It is still used by area farmers to water crops.

Continue on south to Mission Espada. See some of the best remaining examples of the acequia. You'll find San Antonio's early means of irrigation interesting.

Hours

Open 24 hours a day

Cost

Free

Directions

Take S. St. Mary's, south of downtown, to the Mission Trail, beginning on Mission Road. Follow the signs. Obtain a map from any of the Missions.

FORT SAM HOUSTON MUSEUM NATIONAL HISTORIC LANDMARK

Building 123, 1210 Stanley Road
Fort Sam Houston 78234
210-221-1886

Discover Fort Sam Houston

Any history buff's dream. The museum focuses on the history of the U.S. Army, from its arrival in 1845, when Texas joined the union, to our present day. See weapons from flintlock rifles to automatic machineguns, old photographs, helmets, uniforms and much more.

The museum also offers literature on the fort's history. Obtain handouts on the Quadrangle, Geronimo, and other interesting things about Fort Sam Houston.

Outside see a static display of artillery pieces. Ask for more details.

Hours

Closed Mondays, Tuesdays, and federal holidays
Wed. – Sun. . . . . 10 am – 4 pm

Cost

Free

Directions

Located on Stanley Road, Building 123.

HANGER 9/ EDWARD H. WHITE MUSEUM

Brooks Air Force Base
Building 671
210-536-2203 • 210-531-9767 reservations

Museum on flight medicine history

Housed in the Air Force's oldest aircraft hanger, the museum focuses on the history of flight medicine. The museum features a section on flight nurses, early flight instrumentation, test pilots and more.

Brooks Air Force Base developed the food and pressure suits used by astronauts for the space industry.

Hours

Mon. – Fri. . . . . 8 am – 4 pm

Cost

Free

Directions

S.E. Military Dr. and IH-37

HERTZBERG CIRCUS MUSEUM

210 W. Market Street, San Antonio 78205
210-207-7819 • 210-207-7810 Recording

See historical circus memorabilia

Unusual describes the Hertzberg Circus Museum. See items like Tom Thumb's carriage, his violin, and his rifle. Learn about some interesting circus performers. Ever hear of a three-legged man? How about the world's tallest man or fattest woman? Your kids will find this museum fascinating.

Begin with the interesting 30-minute video, then explore the displays. The museum houses a priceless collection of artifacts, over 20,000 circus-related items.

One Saturday a month, the museum invites families to participate in activities: magic shows, juggling acts, mime performances, and mask-making workshops. Call or watch the local newspaper for upcoming events. The museum also makes computers available to children with software the kids will enjoy.

Park the car across the street in the River Bend Parking Garage. The parking garage offers one hour of free parking for museum attendees.

Hours

Mon. – Sat.	10 am – 5 pm
Sunday (Summer only)	1 pm - 5 pm

Cost

Adults	$2.50
Children (3 – 12)	$1
Children under 3	Free
Seniors	$2

Group rates are available

Directions

At the corner of S. Presa and Market.

INSTITUTE OF TEXAN CULTURES

801 South Bowie Street, San Antonio 78205
210-458-2300
210-458-2291 group reservations

Texas folk culture comes alive at this museum

People from many countries settled the great state of Texas. In fact, some 27 different ethnic groups have influenced the present-day culture. Learn more about Texas history and what these people contributed. The museum features a dome show, "Faces and Places of Texas," with a multimedia exhibit of 36 screens. Plan on an hour and forty minutes to see the show.

Part of the University of Texas, the museum was built for the 1968 HemisFair. Docents will explain interesting aspects of exhibits: for example, how cowboys on a cattle drive cooked on the open range. Take a guided tour of the museum with your family. The museum also provides two hours of free parking with admission.

Hours

Closed Mondays, Thanksgiving, and Christmas
Tues. – Sun. . . . . 9 am – 5 pm

Cost

Adults $4
Children (2-12) $2
Seniors 65+ $2
Group rates $2

Directions

Located in HemisFair Park, on Bowie and Durango Streets. Enter on Durango.

LA VILLITA HISTORIC DISTRICT

418 Villita Street, San Antonio 78205
210-207-8610

Visit the shops and plazas, keeping its history in mind

The La Villita Historic District is distinctive in San Antonio's rich history. Known as "San Antonio's Little Village," it originated as one of the first Spanish settlements along the San Antonio River. At La Villita, Santa Ana prepared for the famous battle against the 189 defenders of the Alamo.

The once-humble dwellings of this old Spanish settlement now serve as unique little shops. You will find arts and crafts of all kinds.

In April, La Villita comes alive with the 10-day Fiesta celebration, *A Night in Old San Antonio*. Considered the largest historic preservation festival in the country, the event is a fundraiser for the San Antonio Conservation Society. For the event, La Villita splits into areas of different ethnic foods and music, providing a taste of San Antonio's culture and history. You'll want to participate in this well-organized and popular event.

Hours

Closed Thanksgiving, Christmas, and New Year's Eve
Daily . . . . 10 am – 5 pm

Cost

Free

Directions

Across from the entrance to HemisFair Park near the River Walk. On S. Alamo and Nueva Street.

MEXICAN CULTURAL INSTITUTE
600 HemisFair Park, San Antonio 78205
210-227-0123 • 210-224-8633

Visit the Aztec building in HemisFair Park

San Antonio's Mexican Institute brings Mexican culture to its own doorstep. The Mexican institute promotes close historical, cultural, social, and traditional ties with Mexico. Inviting Mexico's artists and performers to San Antonio, the institute offers cultural experiences open to the public.

The institute offers conferences, performing arts, a movie series, visual arts, and workshops. With these activities, the institute hopes to create a better understanding of the language, literature, history, art, customs, and folklore.

Experience for yourself what this institute has to offer. See the art gallery with visiting artists' works on display. Impressive. Ask for a schedule of their upcoming events.

Hours
Mon. – Fri. . . . . 10am – 5pm

Cost
Free

Directions
In HemisFair Park. Use the entrance on Alamo Street.

McNAY ART MUSEUM

6000 N. New Braunfels, San Antonio 78209
210-824-5368
www.mcnayart.org

San Antonio's classical art museum

Marion Koogler McNay left her beautiful Mediterranean-style home, the surrounding property, her art collection, and part of her wealth to establish this art museum. Opening in 1954 as the first modern art museum in Texas, the museum displays a wonderful art collection. You'll delight in works of the 19th and 20th century great masters: O'Keefe, Van Gogh, Matisse, Picasso, Cezanne, Pollack, Gauguin, and Toulouse-Lautrec.

Stroll the lush landscaped gardens with water fountains, a Japanese garden, fishponds, garden sculptures, and a courtyard. Bring along a picnic lunch.

Be sure to watch for upcoming events and visiting exhibits. The museum hosts works of artists you won't want to miss.

Hours

Closed Thanksgiving, Christmas, and New Year's Eve
Closed Mondays

Tues. – Sat. . . . . 10 am – 5 pm
Sun. . . . . Noon – 5 pm

Cost

(Donations accepted)
Free

Directions

Located at the corner of North New Braunfels Avenue and Austin Highway. Take Broadway north of downtown to Austin Highway.

PIONEER, TRAIL DRIVERS AND TEXAS RANGER MEMORIAL MUSEUM

3805 Broadway, San Antonio 78209
210-822-9011

Honors the Texas Rangers and early pioneers

Stephen F. Austin needed to protect the 300 families he brought here to settle the Texas frontier. Hiring ten men to roam the range and provide protection, he created the first law enforcement agency in North America. Even today, the Texas Rangers make up the strongest law enforcement group in Texas.

See old photographs of famous Texas Rangers hanging on the walls in this fine old museum. Dedicated to the legacy, this museum lets us relive their day. See guns, saddles, and the badges of the legendary men.

The museum also honors the trail drivers who drove some 10,000,000 head of longhorn cattle to markets in the north between 1866 and 1895. See saddles, branding irons, spurs, and barbed wire carried on the trail.

Take note of the building that houses this museum. The rotunda is a miniature replica of the one at the state capitol building in Austin.

Hours
Closed Thanksgiving, Christmas, and New Year's Eve

Summer Mon. – Sat . . . . 10 am – 5 pm
Sunday . . . . Noon–5 pm
Winter Mon. – Sat. . . . . 11 am – 4 pm
Sunday . . . . Noon–4 pm

Cost

Adults $2
Children (4 – 12) (under 4 Free) . . . . $.50
Seniors (55+) $1.50

Directions - Next to the Witte Museum.

SAN ANTONIO'S CHILDREN'S MUSEUM

305 E. Houston Street, San Antonio 78205
210-212-4453

San Antonio's fantastic children's museum

With hands-on exhibits geared for children ages 2-10, the museum will fascinate your kids for hours—parents too. It offers over 80 educational and interesting things to do.

Set up as a miniature San Antonio, the exhibits focus on everyday life such as shopping, going to the doctor, banking, gardening, and constructing buildings and streets. Climb the replica of the H.E.B Science Tree-house or even take a pretend trolley ride around town.

Other fun activities involve recycling, nature, art, and even bubble blowing. A favorite of many is the Teddy Bear Hospital, with opportunities to help teddy bear patients get well.

Family friendly, the museum offers excellent annual memberships that make the museum affordable for everyone. Enjoy one hour of free parking at the Mid-City Garage.

Hours & Costs

Mon. – Friday	9 am – 5 pm
Saturday	9 am – 6 pm
Sunday	Noon – 4 pm
Per person	$4
Members & Children under 2	Free
Annual family membership	$50

Directions - One block from the River Walk on Houston and Navarro Streets.

SAN ANTONIO MUSEUM OF ART

200 W. Jones Avenue, San Antonio
210-978-8100 • 210-829-7262
www.samuseum.org

See the restored old Lone Star Brewery

The largest brewery in Texas at the turn of the century sat vacant for decades until its potential was realized and the building was restored. You'll find this renovated old brewery fascinating. It now houses one of the finest collections of art in the State of Texas and is listed in the National Register of Historic Places.

Ask for a guided tour or visit the museum on your own. You'll enjoy highlights that include Mexican folk art, a Pre-Columbian gallery, Asian art, and ancient art of the antiquities. See paintings of the 1800's, Chinese art, and much more.

New to the museum is the Nelson A. Rockfeller Center for Latin American Art. Be sure to include this in your visit. Stop into the gift shop with art books, jewelry, crafts, and other artistic items. Coming here is a must. The museum is free to the public on Tuesdays from 3 pm – 9 pm.

Hours & Costs

Closed Thanksgiving and Christmas • Closed Mondays

Tuesday	10 am – 9 pm
Wed. – Sat	10 am – 5 pm
Sunday	Noon – 5 pm
Adults	$5
Children (4 – 11)	$1.75
Members & Children under 3	Free
Students/Seniors 65+	$4

Directions - Go North on Broadway to W. Jones St.
Go left. Will be on the right.

SPANISH GOVERNOR'S PALACE

105 Plaza De Armas, San Antonio 78205
210-224-0601

One of the oldest structures in San Antonio

The Spanish Governor's Palace meant domination in the New World. The early Spanish stronghold helped to discourage French ambitions and established a Spanish ruling government. Built for the aristocratic class, many a dignitary stayed here.

Today, the Spanish Governor's Palace opens its doors for a unique experience in early frontier living. Built in 1749, it was luxurious and elegant for its day. You'll find the house restored to its original state, filled with authentic furnishings. Its well-built walls are three-feet thick. Notice the carvings on the front door, depicting the story of Spanish American history. As a registered National Historic Landmark, I'm sure you will find the house interesting.

Hours

Mon. – Sat.	9 am – 5 pm
Sunday	10 am – 5 pm

Cost

Adults	$1
Children under 14	$.50
Children under 7	Free
Seniors	$1

Directions

Located between Commerce and Dolorosa Streets, behind city hall.

STEVES HOMESTEAD

509 King William Street, San Antonio 78204
210-225-5924

Tour home in the Historic King William District

Edward Steves made his fortune operating the local lumber mill. With that fortune, he built a magnificent 3-story house along the San Antonio River in the most prominent part of town. Built in 1876 and restored to its original beauty, the house reflects an interesting era in San Antonio's history.

Out back, the Steves estate includes the River House, the first indoor swimming pool in San Antonio. See the 2-story carriage house, built with a storage room and servant's quarters.

If you love history and old mansions, you'll find the guided tour intriguing. Include the 1-hour tour of this historic home with the self-guided walking tour of the King William Historic District. Maps of the historic district are available at the San Antonio Conservation Society at 107 King William.

Hours

Daily . . . . 10 am – 4:15 pm

Cost

Adults $3
Children under 12 . . . . Free

Directions

Located in the Historic King William District at St. Mary's and King William Streets.

TEXAS TRANSPORTATION MUSEUM
11731 Wetmore Road, San Antonio 78247
210-490-3554

A haven for any train enthusiasts

Focusing on means of surface travel, the 5000-square-foot Texas Transportation Museum makes for a great family outing.

See the fine collection of antique horse-drawn carriages. The museum's unique collections include a horse-drawn fire truck, a Studebaker Carriage, a doctor's carriage, and a Victorian Brougham Carriage.

Inside the museum you will find an old restored train depot from Congress, Texas. Walk though the old steam locomotive, the business car, and the Pullman car you'll find on display. The museum features three working model railroads and an array of classic cars.

"All aboard!" Best of all take a ride on a real standard-gauge train. The museum offers train rides out back on a 1/3-mile track for any guest on Saturday every hour on the hour, between Noon to 3 pm and on Sunday every 45-minutes, between 12:30 pm and 3:30 pm. Rides are free with the admission price, but donations will be accepted.

Hours
Thurs. Sat. and Sun. . . . . 9 am – 4 pm

Cost
Adults $4
Children under 12 . . . . $2
Special rate (2 adults & 5 kids) $10

Directions
Located near the airport. Take 281 north from downtown. Go east on 410. Exit Wetmore Road and go north past the airport.

U.S ARMY
MEDICAL DEPARTMENT MUSEUM

Building 4011
2310 Stanley Road (Building 1046)
Fort Sam Houston 78234
210-221-6358 • 210-226-0265
210-221-6277 group reservations
www.phoenix.nev~ameddmus

Museum on the U.S. Army Medical History

Home of the U.S. Medical Department, the museum focuses on the U.S. Army medical history from the Revolutionary War to Desert Storm. See a collection of Army medical equipment and vehicles including two ambulances from World War II.

You'll enjoy the photographs and displays. Exhibits feature some of the healing practices used by the Army during war and peace. See uniforms and even makeshift medical equipment.

Hours

Closed federal holidays

Tues. – Sat.   . . . . 10 am – 4 pm

Cost

Free

Directions

Fort Sam Houston is located at the corner of
HarryWurzbach and Stanley Road.
Ask at the gate for detailed directions.

YTURRI-EDMUNDS HISTORIC SITE

128 Mission Road, San Antonio 78210
210-534-8237 or 210-224-6163
210-224-6163 San Antonio Conservation Socity

Over 250 years ago, the Spanish missions gave sections of their farmland to Indian tenants. As one of these land grants, the Yturri-Edmunds Historic Site allows us a look at early times in Texas.

Today, the property consists of an 1860's adobe house. Ownership of the house continued in the same family for over a hundred years, until 1961.

See an original 1820's mill, restored in 1972. Running from beneath the house to the mill is a remnant of the old Spanish irrigation system—the acequia.

Two more structures saved by the San Antonio Conservation Society have been move to this site, the 1881 Oge Carriage House and the 1855 Postert House.

Tours are by appointment only. Call the San Antonio Conservation Society well in advance so they can arrange your tour.

Hours

Tours by appointment only

Cost

Adults $3
Children under 12 . . . . Free

Directions

From downtown take S. St. Mary's going south to Mission Road. Turn right and follow Mission Road as it curves to the left. Will be on the corner of Mission and Yellowstone Roads.

Locations

1. Alamo Street Restaurant and Theater
2. Arneson River Theatre
3. Arts! San Antonio
4. Ballet San Antonio
5. Blue Star Arts Complex
6. Carver Community Cultural Art Center
7. Guadalupe Cultural Arts Center
8. Harlequin Dinner Theater
9. Josephine Theater
10. Magik Children's Theater
11. Majestic Performing Arts Center
12. San Antonio Symphony
13. San Pedro Playhouse
14. "Spirit of Healing" by Jesse Treviño Mural at Santa Rosa's Children's Hospital
15. Steven Stoli Playhouse & The Backyard Theater
16. Southwest School of Arts and Crafts

Chapter 4
SAN ANTONIO HAS CULTURE AND TALENT
art, art galleries, operas, symphony and live theaters

ALAMO STREET RESTAURANT AND THEATRE

1150 S. Alamo Street, San Antonio 78204
210-271-7791

Dinner theater in an old historic church

Eat and be merry in this classy old church in the King William District. Listed on the National Register of Historic Places. The church sanctuary and Sunday school classrooms serve as the stage and dining hall. See comedies, dramas, and musicals to melodramas and murder mysteries. Cheer the heroes, boo at the villains, and question the suspicious for a delightful evening. Call for shows playing; many premier, at the Alamo Street Restaurant and Theatre, then travel elsewhere.

Reservations are a must—at least 2 weeks in advance for dinner and show. Celebrate a birthday, an anniversary, or some special occasion. Let them personalize the evening show for you. Tell them of your occasion when your make a reservation.

Use the theatre for social gatherings. Book a party and get a discount for groups over 20. Call for more details. The old church opens for lunch during the week and dinner when a show is playing. Served buffet style, dinners include roast beef, ham, pastas, salads, and the like.

Lunch - Mon. – Fri. .... 11:30 am – 2 pm
Dinner - Fri. and Sat. .... 6 pm – 8 pm
Show - Fri. and Sat. .... 8 pm–10 pm

Adults *(Shows only)* $13
Children (3 – 10) *(Shows only)* $6
Adults *(Dinner and Shows)* $25
Children under 10 *(Dinner and Shows)* .. $12.50

Directions - 1mile south of HemisFair Plaza, .6 mile south of the intersection of S. Alamo and E. Durango.

82

ARNESON RIVER THEATRE

La Villita—on the River Walk

210-207-8610

Amphitheater on the River Walk

Grab a blanket or cushion and join the fun at the Arneson River Theatre, down on the River Walk. From the Arneson Amphitheater, watch a show across the river. See nightly shows during the summer with live music, dance, and a south-of-the-border flair—a must-see for any tourist or local.

Summertime includes shows from the following production companies: the Fiesta Flamenca on Sunday, Monday, and Tuesday nights, Fandango Folkloric Troupe on Wednesday, and Fiesta Rio del Noche on Thursdays, Fridays, and Saturdays.

Purchase tickets in the La Villita Historic District, at the Arneson River Theatre entrance.

Watch for other productions in the winter; performed less often.

Hours

Summer

Nightly . . . . 8:30 pm

Cost

Tickets . . . . $6 - $10

Directions

Enter at La Villita, located between S. Alamo and S. Presa Streets.

ARTS! SAN ANTONIO

222 E. Houston Street, Suite 630
San Antonio 78205
210-226-2891

A presenting company in San Antonio

See their annual production of "Shakespeare in the Park" in the lovely San Antonio Botanical Gardens, free. Enjoy great entertainment such as *The Nutcracker*, Bill Cosby, or *RiverDance*. Their full season includes ballet, classical and chamber music, contemporary dance, and more from around the world.

Claiming no home, Arts of San Antonio stages their productions at different locations—at the Majestic Theater, at other theaters around town, or in parks. Buy tickets for their performances at the ticket office on 222 E. Houston or at any Ticketmaster outlet. Call for a schedule.

Hours

(Ticket Office)
Mon. – Fri. .... 9 am – 4:30 pm

Cost

Tickets range from $10 - $65

Directions

Located downtown on E. Houston between N. St. Mary's and Navarro Streets.

BALLET SAN ANTONIO

4335 Vance Jackson
San Antonio
210-340-0607

San Antonio's got ballet

Attend the ballet school's demonstration and see their students perform. Children begin classes here at early ages. Many eventually become professional dancers. Open to the public; see students at all levels dance with their ballet company. This event is held each May.

The ballet company's performances throughout the year include *The Nutcracker* during the holidays. See it performed in the Cockrell Theatre downtown. Call for their demonstration and performance schedules. For tickets, call Ticketmaster.

Interested in a seeing their school facilities? Ask them for a tour.

Hours

Call for schedule

Cost

(Demonstrations)
Free
Ticket for performances vary

Directions

To get to the studio from downtown, take I-10 West then 410 going east. Exit Vance Johnson and go left. Will be 1 blocks outside the Loop on the left behind McDonalds.

San Antonio Has **Culture And Talent**

BLUE STAR ARTS COMPLEX

1420 S. Alamo Street, San Antonio 78204
210-227-6960
www.blue-star.net

San Antonio's contemporary art community

If you love contemporary art, visit the Blue Star Complex. Old historic warehouses across the river from the King William district now house San Antonio's contemporary art community. See works of local, regional, national, and even international artists. Galleries, such as Art Space, attract art lovers across Texas to their monthly opening.

These warehouses consist of more than art galleries: studios, a restaurant, a theater, and even apartments. The following places highlight the area.

BLUE STAR ART SPACE

116 Blue Star, Building C, 210-227-6960
An art gallery featuring contemporary art.

SAN ANGEL FOLK ART

110 Blue Star, Studio 100, Building B, 210-226-6688
See Mexican folk art.

Hours

Hours to galleries vary
Wed. – Sun. . . . . Noon – 6pm

Cost

Free

Directions

Five minutes south of downtown. Take S. Alamo south 1.5 miles. It's south of the San Antonio River.

CARVER COMMUNITY CULTURAL CENTER

226 N. Hackberry Street, San Antonio 78202
210-207-7211

San Antonio's successful multicultural community center

Big name artists like Ella Fitzgerald, Duke Ellington, Count Basie, Louie Armstrong, and "Dizzy" Gillespie walked through these doors. The Carver Community Cultural Art Center traces it historic roots back before desegregation. It started in 1905 as a cultural center for the black community in San Antonio and now stands as a national model of a multicultural center.

Today, the Carver Community Cultural Center sponsors an annual season of performing and visual arts. Every year, it features more than 50 performances, 24 art exhibitions, and numerous classes for young artists. Teaching everything from dance to ceramics, the center supports numerous arts and cultural activities in the community.

Tour the center. Learn more about its rich cultural heritage and what it offers the community. Tours last approximately 20 minutes.

Hours

Mon. – Fri. . . . . 8 am – 5 pm

Cost

Free

Directions

Take E. Houston, going east from downtown to N. Hackberry and turn left (south). Will be between Center and Gibbs Street.

GUADALUPE CULTURAL ARTS CENTER

1300 Guadalupe Street, San Antonio 78207
210-271-3151

San Antonio's Hispanic cultural arts center

The Guadalupe Cultural Arts Center is recognized nationally as a huge success. Dedicated to the arts and culture of the Chicano, Latino, and Native American people, this center's activities involve all the arts: dance, literature, media, music, theater, and visual arts.

Tour the center. See the historic theater, the gallery, the dance studio, and the art gallery. The 1.5 hour tour offers insights in to the area's history and the center's 18 years of success.

Visit the art gallery and the gift shop. Return for a performance at the amphitheater or a concert. Popular, well-known annual events, such as the Tejano Conjunto Festival celebrate Tejano sounds. Attend their Inter-American Bookfair and Literary Festival, gathering Spanish literature from around the world. CineFestival highlights up-and-coming Hispanic films.

Hours (Center)

Mon. – Fri. . . . . 10 am – 6 pm

Cost (Tour)

Free

Directions

Take I-10 to I-35N, exit UTSA Downtown Campus. Go left on Durango, then left on Frio. Go right on Guadalupe (the next light). Cross a bridge and down two lights to Brazos. It's on the corner of Guadalupe and Brazos.

HARLEQUIN DINNER THEATER

Building 2652 Harney Road
Fort Sam Houston 78208
210-221-5953

Army base dinner theater open to the public

Get your reservation now. Tickets go quickly at the Harlequin Dinner Theater. Call a week or two in advance for your reservation. Producing plays for 24 years, the theater is located at Fort Sam Houston, a military base accessible to the public.

Dinner includes bread, all-you-can-eat soup and salad, a choice of 4 entrees and 3 desserts, and a drink. Entrees include roast beef, chicken, and fish dishes.

Simply **Wait 'til Dark** for favorites like Agatha Christi's murder mysteries, **I Hate Hamlet** and **The Man Who Came to Dinner.** The theater produces eight plays a year and offers a season pass. It opens for seating at 6:15 pm; dinner is served at 7 pm. The show begins at 8 pm.

Hours

Wednesday, Thursday, Friday, and Saturday evenings

Cost (includes dinner)

Wed. and Thursday $20.95
Fri. and Sat. $22.95

Directions

Accessible to the public, Fort Sam Houston is 10 minutes from downtown San Antonio. Take I-35N and exit Walters Street. Go left on Walters Street. It will take you onto the base. Walters Street changes to Scott Street. Follow to Harney Road and go right. Will be one-half block down on the right.

JOSEPHINE THEATER

339 W. Josephine Street
San Antonio 78215
210-734-4646

Local theater flaunts local talent

All musicals—see five a year at the Josephine Theater. Many are award winning. Enjoy favorites like *My Fair Lady, 42nd Street,* and *Crazy for You*. The theater, built in 1945, features an art deco architecture.

On occasions, performances include dramatic classics. Call for their program schedule. The theater is situated near restaurants.

Hours

Fri. and Sat.	8:15 pm
Sunday	2:30 pm

Cost

Adults	$18
Seniors	$16
Students	$12
Children under 12	$8

Directions

Located between Broadway and N. St. Mary's Streets. From downtown, take Broadway north past I-35 to Josephine and go left.

MAGIK CHILDREN'S THEATER

420 S. Alamo Street
San Antonio 78205
210-227-2751

A top-notch children's theater

Like magic, even moms and dads get caught up in the fun. See what's playing at the Magik Theater. Better yet, get a season pass. Based on popular well-known children's literature, their plays will delight the whole family.

Let the kids read the book then see the play—like **The Tale of a Fourth Grade Nothing** or **The Grinch**. Other favorite performances include originals like the **The Phantom of the Alamo**—a must-see. Ask to be on the mailing list to keep up with their season's programming.

Acting classes for children and summer camps are available. Call for details.

Hours

Tues. & Thurs.. . . . . 9:30 am and 11:30 am
Wednesday . . . . 10:30 am
Friday . . . . 9:30 am, 11:30 am, & 7 pm
Saturday . . . . 1 pm, 4 pm, & 7 pm

Cost

Adults $8
Children (3 - 17) $6
Children under 3 . . . . $2
Seniors 65+ $7

Directions

Located in HemisFair Park at S. Alamo and Nueva.

MAJESTIC PERFORMING ARTS CENTER

230 E. Houston
San Antonio 78205
210-226-3333 Tickets
210-223-4343 Times & Prices

San Antonio's elegant theater

At the Majestic Performing Arts Center, see San Antonio's finest—productions and theater. Presenting arts include a Broadway series, concerts, ballets, children's theater, Tejano music awards, and big-name performers. Majestic aptly describes this atmospheric theater, one of only few left. Architect John Eberson's design adds elegance to any performance. Opened in 1929, the Majestic brought air-conditioning to San Antonio. Recently restored, the theater remains San Antonio's chief center for social affairs. See a performance to see this theater.

Tours of the Majestic Theater are offered. Call Las Casa (210-223-4343) for times and prices.

Hours
(Box Office)

Mon. – Sat. . . . . 10 am – 5 pm

Cost
Vary according to the performance

Directions

On E. Houston between St. Mary's and Navarro Streets.

SAN ANTONIO SYMPHONY

222 East Houston St. #200
San Antonio 78205
210-554-1010
www.sasymphony.org

San Antonio's symphony relates to its community

The symphony got its start —June 12, 1939—
with a gathering of music lovers at the Sunken Garden
Theater. Now celebrating 60 years of community
performances, the symphony continues to move
forward with full seasons of educational, classical,
pops, family, and outreach concerts, over a hundred
concerts each year. Enjoy the diversity their
community-minded programs offer, from Beethoven
to Dance Festivals. Holiday favorites include *Handel's
Messiah, The Nutcracker,* Humperdinck's *Hansel
and Gretel, A Night in Old Vienna.*

The Instrument Petting Zoo, part of the family
Interactive Classics, allows hands-on experiences for
your child. Handle and attempt to play instruments
with a musician's supervision. A Family Pass costs
$140. Call for details.

Hours

Call for the season schedule

Cost

Prices vary for packages and performances

Directions

The San Antonio Symphony performs most of
its concerts in the beautiful Majestic Performing Arts
Center located at 230 E. Houston. Check performing
schedules for locations.

SAN PEDRO PLAYHOUSE

800 W. Ashby, San Antonio
210-733-7258

Local talent performs classics and originals

See musical favorites such as the **Little Shop of Horrors, The King and I,** and **Man of La Mancha** at San Antonio's oldest community theater. Located in the city's oldest park. The San Pedro Playhouse's original works, like the comedy, **Daddy's Dying, Who's Got the Will**, about a wealthy Texas rancher who dies and leaves his heirs a bottle of live potion complete with the formula, still delights audiences.

Open to community involvement, the theater offers interactive plays in schools, like **Snow White and the Seven Dwarfs.** Children get opportunities to develop an interest in theater.

Hours

Box office hours

Tues. – Fri. .... 10am – 5pm

Cost

Adults .... $17 - 20
Children (under 8) $8
Students (under 25) $11
Seniors .... $2 discount

Directions

Traveling north on I-35 on the north side of downtown, get in the left-hand lane and continue on I-35 as it splits from I-10. Take the first exit, San Pedro Avenue, and go left. Continue on San Pedro Avenue for 1.5 miles to Ashby and go left. The parking lot will be on the left.

"SPIRIT OF HEALING"
by Jesse Treviño
MURAL AT SANTA ROSA CHILDREN'S HOSPITAL
Houston Street—across from Market Square

Fantastic mural on local children's hospital

Perhaps you'll meet the artist of this masterpiece as he lunches across the street. See this impressive mural entitled "Spirit of Healing" on the side of the Santa Rosa Children's Hospital. Created by a famous well-known artist, Jesse Treviño, the mural, 90 feet high and 40 feet wide is one of the largest in North America and contains over 150,000 pieces of hand-cut ceramic tile.

Overlooking Milam Park, the mural depicts a child holding a dove with a guardian angel and a cross in the background. To portray the innocence of youth, affection, and gentleness, the artist used his 10-year-old son as a model. The dove symbolizes peace, love, freedom, and spirituality. Make this part of your sightseeing in San Antonio.

The artist, Jesse Treviño often lunches at Mi Tierra Café at Market Square. With a little luck, you may see him there.

Hours
Drive by and stop anytime.

Cost
Free

Directions
On the side of the Santa Rosa Children's Hospital,

STEVEN STOLI PLAYHOUSE AND THE BACKYARD THEATER

11838 Wurzbach, San Antonio, 210-408-0116

A theater for children and a theater for grown-ups

Children's plays sell out quickly at the Backyard Theater. Reservations for an annual favorite, **Frosty's New Hat Adventures**, start in September. The Backyard Theater's list of dandy productions include plays like **Humpty-Dumpty's Pumpkin Patch, The Three Pigs, The City Mouse and The Country Mouse, Aladdin,** and **Turkey in the Store**—a Thanksgiving special. Bring your blanket and wear comfortable clothes, kids sit on the floor. Ask to be on their mailing list.

For the grown-ups, the Playhouse seats about 80 people and features terrific shows. Enjoy the Playhouse's great variety of shows. Watch plays like **Odd Couple— a female version, Match Makers, Driving Miss Daisy, Watching for MacArthur, War of the World** and **Social Security**. Year-round performances, with local talent.

Backyard Theater Hours & Costs

Tuesday	10 am
Saturday	10 am and Noon
Children	$4.50
Adults	$3.75

Playhouse Hours & Costs

Friday	8 pm
Saturday	7:30 pm
Sunday	2:30 pm
Adults	$16
Seniors & Groups 20+	$13

Directions - In the Elms Shopping Ctr, center of the second floor. Take I-10N to Wurzbach exit and go right (north) to Lockhill-Selma. Will be on the corner.

SOUTHWEST SCHOOL OF ARTS AND CRAFTS

300 Augusta Street, San Antonio 78205
210-224-1848

A unique combination of contemporary art at an historic site

Only a few professional-level art schools in our nation such as the Southwest School of Arts and Crafts teach as a non-degree-granting institute. Housed in the old Ursuline Academy for girls built in 1843, the school offers fun contemporary art classes for everyone, including children. It recently opened its Navarro campus which quadrupled its exhibition space.

The center gives an interesting tour of the historic buildings that lasts approximately 20 minutes. You will want to visit the art galleries: the Emily Edwards Gallery and the Ursuline Gallery, featuring works of visiting artists, students, instructors, and artists-in-residence.

Eat lunch at the Copper Kitchen Restaurant, serving lunch weekdays from 10:30 am to 2 pm. Be sure to browse in the gift shop with unique art and craft items for sale—another fun thing to do.

Special events such as lectures, concerts, and gallery openings invite public attendance. In April, you will enjoy viewing the arts and crafts from all over the United States during the Fiesta Art Fair. See ceramics, furniture, jewelry, paintings, photographs, and other art.

Hours - (Closed major holidays)

Mon. – Fri. . . . . 8:30am – 5pm
Saturaday . . . . 10 am – 5 pm

Cost - Free

Directions - At the corner of Navarro and Augusta across from the enchilada-red Central Library.

Locations

1. Brooks School of Aerospace Medicine
2. Heard Ranch Roundup
3. Goodwill Industries
4. Lightning Ranch
5. Love Creek Apple Orchard
6. Pape's Pecan House
7. Promised Land Barnyard
8. San Antonio LightHouse for the Blind
9. Spirits of San Antonio Tour
10. Southern Cavern Adventure Tour
11. True Women Tours I

Chapter 5
TOURS AND MORE
special interests, field trips, group tours

BROOKS SCHOOL OF AEROSPACE MEDICINE

Human Systems Center

Brooks Air Force Base
San Antonio 78235
210-536-3234

Only for group tours, call well in advance. Brooks School of Aerospace Medicine offers a popular tour for school groups, church groups, scouts, and out-of-towners, with groups of 10 or more. See where John Glenn trained for his flight in space. Tour includes the Human Systems Center's Armstrong Laboratory, the centrifuge, altitude chambers, and the flight school for nurses. Wear comfortable shoes.

Hours

Call for details and a month in advance

Cost

Free

Directions

On Brooks Air Force Base

GOODWILL INDUSTRIES

3830 Pleasanton Road
San Antonio 78221
210-924-8581

See what your donations of used items do for the community

Visit the largest Goodwill Industries in the state of Texas—doing over $5 million worth of business a year. They serve thousands of disabled people, placing many in regular employment. Take the 45-minute tour and get a first-hand look at how donations from the community change lives. Time spent here will be positive and upbeat; you'll leave with a new outlook on their purposes. Call and schedule a time to go.

Hours

(Tour can be arranged)

Mon. – Fri. . . . . 9 am – 3 pm

Cost

Free

Directions

From Interstate 35 South, take the Military Drive exit and go east to Pleasanton Road. Go south. Will be past McDonald's.

HEARD RANCH ROUNDUP

P.O. Box 63, Fredericksburg 78624
210-824-3324 • 800-658-3773

Watch cowboys work cattle on a working ranch

In 1939, Cyrus Heard began ranching in the picturesque countryside of Fredericksburg, Texas, now one of our nation's fastest-growing tourist spots. Heard's grandson, a seventh generation Texas rancher, owns and operates the ranch. Using up-to-date technology, he raises high quality Hereford cattle on the 10,000 acre ranch.

The Texas Hill Country Ranch affords guests opportunities to see authentic cattle roundups, roping, and branding as real cowboys perform duties on a working ranch. Other enjoyable events include a country hayride, gun-fighting dramas, early morning campfire breakfasts, and visits to the historic 1893 Morris Ranch Schoolhouse, that serves as ranch headquarters. Afterwards, join the cowboys around a campfire for a chuckwagon barbecue supper: brisket, slaw, and beans with all the fixings. Activities at the ranch cater any age group.

Hours - Arrange for group tour

Cost - Varies according to group size

Directions

Take I-10 W towards Kerrville, exit US 87 to downtown Fredericksburg and turn left on Main Street. Take Main Street approximately 1.5 miles to N. Adams Street on Highway 16 and go left. Drive about 12 miles to the Morris Ranch Road; go right. Continue 2.4 miles until you see the Morris Ranch Schoolhouse on the right before the Pedernales River. Watch for signs for Heard Ranch.

LIGHTNING RANCH

818 FM 1283
Pipe Creek 78063
830-510-4136
www.lightninranch.com

Enjoy a day of activities on a working ranch

See a family owned and operated working ranch in the heart of the Hill Country. Let their staff present your group, family or anyone with a day that includes horseback rides, hayrides, campfire roasts, trick roping, and western dancing. Learn to rope cattle, groom a horse, or be a blacksmith. The ranch offers guest overnight accommodations and overnight trail rides too. Call for more information. Only 30 minutes from San Antonio.

Hours

Arrange for a group tour

Cost

Varies according to the group's size

Directions

From San Antonio, take Hwy. 16 North. When you reach Pipe Creek turn left at the yellow light on to FM 1283. Go 7/10 mile and the ranch is on your right.

LOVE CREEK APPLE ORCHARDS, NATURE, AND BIRDING TOURS

112 Broadway
Medina 78055
210-589-2588 • 800-449-0882

Visit an apple orchard in the Hill Country

Check in at the Cider Mill and Country Store in downtown Medina before heading for the ranch tour. Delicious apple goodies of all kinds will get you in the spirit of this great adventure: fresh apples, sweet cider, apple pies, and apple products of all kinds.

Continue on to the apple orchards. Located in the heart of the scenic hill country, the 2000-acre ranch pioneered the Texas apple industry. You will see 14 different varieties of dwarf apple trees and the manufacturing of over 50 different apple items like jellies, jams, sauces, and butters. Love Creek Orchards is famous for their wonderful apples, apple pies, and apple ice cream. They feature apple tours year-round by reservations only with a minimum of 25 people. Tours also include apple cider and cookies. Ask about the sack lunch that they can provide for your group, making for a great picnic.

Remember to come back in October for the **"Great Hill Country Pumpkin Patch."** Your kids will enjoy picking a pumpkin for the holidays. Treat your family to this fun occasion.

Love Creek Orchards offers more than apple tours. Participate in one of the nature walks and birding tours that take you along Love Creek. Best time for the nature walk is in late October through mid-December. Enjoy learning about the fauna and flora indigenous to the Hill Country and the interesting geology of the area.

Take a birding tour in one of the best areas for finding interesting birds in South Texas. See birds like the golden-cheeked warbler, the black-capped vireo, the blue grosbeak, eastern bluebirds, painted and indigo buntings, to name a few. Call for more details.

Hours

Office Hours

Mon. – Fri. . . . . 9 am – 5 pm

Store

Mon. – Sat. . . . . 9 am – 5 pm
Sunday . . . . 10 am – 5 pm

Cost

(Discounts are available for school groups)

Apple orchards tours

Per person (minimum of 25 people) $4

Nature walking tours

Per person (includes sack lunch) $25

Birding tours

Per person (minimum of 6 people/lunch) $15

Directions

Love Creek Orchards is located 60 miles northwest of San Antonio. Take I-10 West to Boerne. Exit Highway 46. Go left on Highway 46 and then right on Highway 16. Turn right at the light and continue 13 miles to Medina. Follow the signs for the Cider Mill. The ranch is 10 miles from Medina on Ranch Road 337. Will be on the right side of the road. Drive through the gate to the first house. The tour will begin here.

PAPE'S PECAN HOUSE

101 S. 123 Bypass
Seguin 78155
830-379-7442 • 888-688-7273

See pecan orchards and processing facilities

Family owned and operated, the famous Pape's Pecan House resides in the heart of the pecan orchard country. Pape's Pecan House processes an amazing 10,000 pounds of pecans every day. Open year-round, see how the Papes raise and process so many nuts. Take the walking tour of the orchards and facilities; you will find it enjoyable.

Pape's Pecan House makes pecans available for purchase. Buy them by the pound or by the truckload; they are the freshest available. Pape's Pecan House also retails other nuts, fruits, and candies. Plan to stock up. Ask for the recipe for Pape's Pralines.

This unique place prides itself on its fantastic collection of nutcrackers. They claim to have over 3000 different kinds from all over the world: hand-carved toy soldiers, Betel Cutters, and much more. Imagine seeing one over 6 feet tall.

Hours

Mon. – Fri. . . . . 8 am – 5 pm
Saturday . . . . 8 am – 1 pm

Cost

Free

Directions

Located 35 miles east of San Antonio. Take I-10 east approximately 30 miles to the 610-Mile Exit and go south to the 4th traffic light. Will be on the corner of 90A (Court Street) and 123 Bypass.

PROMISED LAND BARNYARD

Route 3 Box 197D
Floresville 78114
830-216-7182 ex. 105

Visit a working dairy farm

Feel like part of the family when you visit Promise Land Barnyard and spend an afternoon in the wholesome country atmosphere. Take the tour of a working dairy and creamery. See how they milk the Jersey cows, bottle the milk in old-fashioned glass bottles, make Supremely Creamy Ice Cream and other dairy products.

The farm offers hayrides through the rolling hills, a petting barn where kids get close and personal with the animals, and miniature golf on the 9-hole course. Be sure to browse through the gift shop, with country crafts and antique dairy items. Wear comfortable casual clothing and athletic shoes for this adventure.

Before going home, dine in the restaurant delicious home-cooked food. Have a great day in the country.

Hours

Mon. – Sat.	10 am – 4 pm
Sunday	10 am – 4 pm

Cost

Tour / person	$4
Tour & hayride / per person	$5

Directions

From downtown San Antonio, take I-37 south to Highway 181. Go south to Floresville and turn right (west) on Highway 97. Continue for 3.5 miles. Watch for the big red barn on the right.

SAN ANTONIO LIGHTHOUSE FOR THE BLIND

2305 Roosevelt
San Antonio 78210
210-533-5195

Tour the industrial plant and rehabilitation center

Arrange to take a tour of a light industrial plant with modified equipment and a rehabilitation area for the blind. As an agency for the Texas Commission for the Blind, the LightHouse evaluates and trains as well as teaches literacy skills. Enjoy a better understanding of their operation and how people with visual problems can develop their abilities. Group tours last approximately 1.5 hours. Wear comfortable shoes, you will be walking. Call at least two weeks in advance. *Note:* Children need to be 7 years old or older for the tour.

Hours
(Arrange for a tour)
Mon. – Fri. . . . . .7:30 am – 4:30 pm

Cost
Free

Directions

From downtown, take St. Mary's south—it will turn into Roosevelt. Will be past the Riverside Golf Course.

SOUTHERN CAVERN ADVENTURE TOUR

26495 Natural Bridge Cavern Road
Natural Bridge Caverns 78266
210-651-6101
www.naturalbridgetexas.com/caverns

Go spelunking in huge caverns

Groups up to ten people can arrange to explore the undeveloped rooms and passages of the Natural Bridge Caverns. Experience what it was like to discover the unknown, there's nothing commercial about this tour.

The tour through these caverns is physically demanding. Be in good physical shape. No one under 13 is allowed on the tour. Guests will be outfitted with helmets, lights, coveralls, gloves, and fanny packs with water and snacks. Be sure to wear shoes with lots of traction and ankle support. Tennis shoes aren't recommended. Cameras are allowed.

Enter the caverns through the original shafts used by explorers in 1968. You'll be lowered 160 feet to the cavern floor. Or you can chose to enter the shaft through a walk-in tunnel. The trail through the caverns is the one used created by the original explorers.

You will return muddy, so bring an extra change of clothes. Showers and lockers will be provided.

Hours
Call for tour schedule

Cost (Tour prices)
Walk-in entrance $75
Entrance Shaft drop-in $100
Drop-in and walk out only $50

Directions
Located between San Antonio and New Braunfels, take I-35 north and exit #175.

SPIRITS OF SAN ANTONIO TOUR
210-493-2454

Enjoy an evening with
San Antonio's authority of spooks

Let Docia Williams, author of two historical guides to haunted places in Texas, take you to some of the spookiest places in San Antonio. Open for groups only of 30 or more. Smaller groups may join others if room is available. This is a popular activity, particularly around Halloween.

Tours are at night, last 3 hours, and include dinner at a haunted restaurant.

Hours
Call for meeting places, times, and reservations

Cost
Tour (includes dinner) . . . . $38 each

TRUE WOMEN TOURS

Seguin Convention and Visitors Bureau
427 N. Austin St.
Seguin 78155
800-580-7322

Tour the city made popular by the novel, *True Women*

Relive tales—the history and secrets of the frontier town of Sequin during the days of the Republic of Texas, as found in Janice Woods Windle's popular novel, **True Women.** Now a mini-series. Enjoy the tour with bridges much like those found in the movie **Bridges of Madison County.** Take a group tour provided with a step-on guide or the self-guided driving tour—exteriors only—with guide maps available at the visitor center. Plan to wear comfortable walking shoes and casual clothing. The tour lasts approximately 3 hours.

Hours

Group tour by appointment only

Cost

Guided tour

Guide for the tour $50
Per person $4

Directions

From downtown San Antonio, take I-10 East to Sequin—32 miles. Exit 609. Go right on Austin Street. The tourist information center will be on the left, before the Texas Theater, at the intersection of Austin and Ireland Streets.

Locations

1. Alamo Village
2. Alamo Pedicab Company
3. Crystal Ice Palace
4. Diamond W. Longhorn Ranch
5. Embassy Skate Center
6. Grayline Lone Star Trolley Tour
7. Grayline Tours of San Antonio
8. Japanese Tea Garden
9. Kiddie Park
10. Laser Quest
11. Lone Star Trolley Tour
12. Malibu Castle & Malibu Grand Prix
13. Retama Park
14. Ripley's Believe It or Not / Plaza of Wax
15. Scobee Planetarium
16. Splashtown
17. Texas Trolley Hop
18. VIA San Antonio Streetcars Locations

Chapter 6
AMUSEMENT PARKS AND ATTRACTIONS
City Tours, Trolleys, and Streetcars

ALAMO VILLAGE

P.O. Box 528, Brackettville 78832
830-563-2580

Movie making in West Texas

"Out in the middle of nowhere" takes on new meaning as you drive north of Brackettville on Highway 674. Keep going, seven more miles. You'll see where John Wayne recreated early frontier days in his movie **The Alamo**. To do so, he built an authentic replica of the Alamo. See this replica.

Used in moviemaking, the filming site includes a western frontier town with all that you'd expect to find: a jail, a hotel, a saloon, a bank, a general store, a livery stable, and more. Other movie favorites filmed here include **Lonesome Dove, Bandolero,** and **Streets of Laredo.**

Walk the streets, browse the gift shop, and visit the John Wayne Museum. See musicals and gunfights in the streets.

Go when the weather is cooler—October through April. Wear casual, comfortable clothes and shoes. Pack a cooler with food; eating establishments are few and far between.

Hours

Closed the week of Christmas

Daily . . . . 9 am – 6 pm

Cost

Adults $7
Children (11 - 6) $4
Children under 5 . . . . Free

Directions

From San Antonio take Highway 90 West 125 miles to Brackettville. Go 7 miles north on 674.

114

ALAMO PEDICAB COMPANY

151 W. Hermine Street
San Antonio 78212
210-889-0199

Get anywhere you want to go downtown with an Alamo Pedicab

Call an Alamo Pedicab and get around quickly. Go from any hotels to restaurants, to museums, or any other destination in no time without all the hassles of parking. Sit back and enjoy a pleasant ride while your friendly bike-pedaling chauffeur entertains you with historic tidbits.

Arrange to use pedicabs for other occasions: parties, weddings, romantic evenings, or any fun downtown excursion. Call and ask for more details.

Hours

Daily . . . . 8 am–Midnight

Cost

Alamo Pedicabs work on tips

Directions

Call for a ride anywhere in the downtown area.

CRYSTAL ICE PALACE
12332 W I-10 Site #12
San Antonio 78320
210-696-0006

San Antonio's only ice skating rink

Cheap skates for any cheap ice skater. Skate Monday or Tuesday nights from 7 pm – 9:30 pm for $2 at this well-run establishment with a friendly staff who like to assist patrons. Even small children can enjoy skating. The Crystal Ice Palace offers skates as small as a child's size eight and convenient skating hours day or evening.

Skates rent for $2 or bring your own.

Sign up for lessons, for your birthday party, or attend special events, like the Fiesta Competition that's held in April.

Hours

Mon. – Thurs.	11 am – 5 pm
	7 pm – 9:30 pm
Friday	11 am – 5 pm
	7:30 pm – Midnight
Saturday	1 pm – 5 pm
	7:30 pm – Midnight
Sunday	1 pm – 5 pm
	7 pm – 9:30 pm

Cost

Adults	$7
Children (4 – 12)	$5.90
Children (3 and under)	Free
Seniors	$5.90

Directions

Located at I-10 and De Zavala Road.

DIAMOND W. LONGHORN RANCH CHUCK WAGON DINNER & COWBOY SHOW

18725 Bandera Road
Helotes 78023
210-695-4888

An evening out on the country

It's like a dinner theater; but the show takes place outdoor on a ranch. Enjoy a tasty chuck wagon supper with real pit barbecue (brisket, smoked turkey, and sausage) and the traditional fixings. Listen to old time cowboy music and see a longhorn do tricks. The show also includes trick roping and a melodrama.

Play a game of horseshoes or washer tossing. Visit the ranch's general store and gift shop. Reservations required. As they put it, " the ranch is only 35 minutes from downtown San Antonio by car or two days on a cattle drive".

Hours

Call for show schedule

Cost

Adults $25
Children 4-12 . . . . $13.50
Children under 3 . . . . Free

Directions

From San Antonio, take I-10 north to Loop 1604. Go south, on 1604 to Hwy. 16 North.

EMBASSY SKATE CENTER

606 Embassy Oaks
San Antonio 78216
210-495-2525

San Antonio's new roller skating rink

Skate with a view. The Embassy Skate Center's large windows make it a unique place to go skating.

Family oriented, the rink offers an afternoon of fun at a reasonable admission that includes the skates if you don't plan to bring your own. Children ages four and older will enjoy the activities. With refreshments and video games the center provides a great place for birthday parties. Or sign up for skating classes and private lessons. Call for more details.

Hours

(Extended hours in the summer)

Daily . . . . 3 pm – 6 pm
Sat. and Sun. . . . . 1 pm – 5 pm
Fri. and Sat. . . . . 7:30 pm – 11 pm

Cost

(Includes skates)

Weekdays $3.50
Weekends $5.00

Directions

From downtown, take Highway 281 N. and exit Bitters Road. Go left on Bitters to the first stop light then left on Embassy Row. Located behind the Embassy 14 Movie Theater.

GRAYLINE OF SAN ANTONIO
LONE STAR TROLLEY TOURS

217 Alamo Plaza, San Antonio
210-226-1706

See San Antonio on a trolley

Hop on the trolley all you want, all day long. Board a replica, turn-of-the-century trolley for a personal guided tour of historic San Antonio. When the tour is over, you'll have an idea of what the city offers. Trolleys leave every 30 minutes with stops along the way. Tickets include "off and on" privileges good for the day. Simply catch the next trolley and continue on with the tour. Go early; plan to spend most of the day. You'll find this to be an excellent way to see downtown.

The trolley will stop at the following: the Alamo, the Hertzberg Circus Museum, Arneson River Theatre, La Villita, Yanaguana River Cruise, Institute of Texan Cultures, Tower of the Americas at HemisFair Park, Mission San Jose, Mission Concepcion, Lone Star Buckhorn Museum, King William Historic District, San Fernando Cathedral, Spanish Governor's Palace, and Market Square. Have fun sightseeing San Antonio.

Hours & Costs

Daily	10 am – 5:45 pm
Adults	$9.50
Children (3 – 12)	$4
Children under 3	Free

Directions

Across from the Alamo, at Ripley's Believe It or Not.

GRAYLINE TOURS OF SAN ANTONIO

217 Alamo Plaza, Suite B, San Antonio 78205
210-226-1706 • 800-472-9546

Enjoy one of these tours

Want to see more than just San Antonio? San Antonio Gray Line Tours offers a wide variety of tours to choose from—each having a particular focus. Tours include Austin, the Texas Hill Country, and Mexico.

Here's a brief sampling of what they offer. Ask about the one that interests you.

The Mission Trail
The Alamo and the Spanish Colonial Missions

San Antonio Sampler
Highlights, Homes, and History

Alamo City Grand Tour
A combination tour plus the Yanaguana River Cruise

Texas Hill Country Escape
LBJ Homesites and Texas Countryside

Tales of Two Cities
Laredo, Texas and Nuevo Laredo, Mexico

Experience Austin
The Texas Capitol

Tours depart from and return to the Alamo Plaza. Or arrange to be picked up and dropped off at your hotel. The cost and length of each tour varies. Some tours leave as early as 8:30 am and the latest returns at 6:30 pm. Prices range between $22 and $38 for an adult and $11 to $19 for children under 12. Lunch is not included in the tour.

JAPANESE TEA GARDEN

3800 N. St. Mary's Street
San Antonio 78212
210-736-9534

Enjoy the garden's serenity

Creating something this unique out of an old rock quarry was a novel idea. See a Japanese garden, with winding pebbled walkways, stone bridges, tranquil pools, and even a 60-foot waterfall. Once supplying limestone for the State Capitol Building in Austin, the old quarry was built in 1917 with prison labor. Now open after extensive renovations, the garden makes a delightful place to visit.

After the Japanese attack on Pearl Harbor, the garden's name changed to the Chinese Sunken Garden. The city finally restored its original name in 1983. Notice the Chinese-looking entrance; it now reminds us of those days.

Take the kids. They will enjoy the stroll. Wear comfortable athletic shoes. You'll climb lots of steps and pathways but will find it inaccessible to strollers.

Hours

Open 24 hour

Cost

Free

Directions

At the northwestern edge of Brackenridge Park.

KIDDIE PARK

3015 Broadway
San Antonio 78209
210-824-4351

Small outdoor amusement park for younger children

Visit the oldest amusement park in the United States. Open year round, weather permitting, Kiddie Park's rides will be a hit with any kids ages 2 to 12. Enjoy traditional amusement park rides, like a roller coaster, a Ferris wheel, a merry-go-round, boat rides, airplane rides, cars, and more. Built in 1918, the original merry-go-round continues to operate. There are arcade games, too.

Concession stands add to the fun or bring along a cooler of food for a picnic. Parking is free. Park either on Avenue B or on Broadway.

Hours

Daily . . . . 10 am – dark

Cost

1 ticket . . . . $.80
5 tickets $3.85
Unlimited rides/person $6.45

Directions

Located on the corner of Broadway and Mulberry. From downtown, simply take Broadway north towards Brackenridge Park.

LASER QUEST

606 Embassy Oaks, San Antonio 78216
210-499-4400

Play a modern game of tag

Imagine yourself wandering through this awesome maze, your heart pounding as you seek out your opponent in this incredible hi-tech game of tag. You're surrounded with action as the fun intensifies. You aim; you fire; you're fired upon.

Your family will find this an unforgettable adventure. Anyone can play the game—if you're big enough to wear the laser pack (children ages 6 or older). Games last approximately 20 minutes.

Play laser tag for your birthday party, with corporate groups, clubs, churches, and scout troops. It offers team-building experiences. Ask about customizing the game. Remember to wear comfortable clothes and athletic shoes. You'll see what computers have done to a simple game of tag. Ask about memberships that include discounts at other local attractions and eateries in the area, special game times and rates.

Hours

Sun.–Thur. .... 2 pm – 10 pm
Fri. – Sat. .... 3 pm – Midnight

Cost

Per game $6.50

Directions

Behind the Embassy 14 Movie Theater on Highway 281 and Bitters Road. From downtown, take Highway 281 N. and exit Bitters Road. Go left on Bitters to the first stop light then left on Embassy Row.

LONE STAR TROLLEY TOUR

217 Alamo Plaza, San Antonio
210-226-1706
(Boarding and tickets from Ripley's Believe It or Not)

San Antonio in a nutshell

Board a replica, turn-of-the-century trolley for a personal guided tour of historic San Antonio. Tours begin downtown, across from the Alamo at the Ripley's Believe It or•Not and the Plaza Theater of Wax. Trolleys leave every 30 minutes. Tickets include "off and on" privileges good for the day. Simply catch the next trolley and continue on with the tour. Go early; plan to spend most of the day. You'll find this to be an excellent way to see downtown.

You'll enjoy visiting the following: the Alamo, the Hertzberg Circus Museum, Arneson River Theatre, La Villita, Yanaguana River Cruise, Institute of Texan Cultures, Tower of the the Americas at HemisFair Park, Mission San Jose, Mission Concepcion, Lone Star Buckhorn Museum, King William Historic District, San Fernando Cathedral, Spanish Governor's Palace, and Market Square. Have fun sightseeing San Antonio.

Hours & Costs

Summer hours extend until 6 pm

Daily . . . . 8 am – 5 pm

Adults $9.50
Children (3 – 12) $4.00
Children under 3 . . . . Free

Directions

Across from the Alamo.

MALIBU CASTLE AND MALIBU GRAND PRIX

3330 Cherryridge, San Antonio 78320
210-341-6664 Miniature golf
210-341-2500 Grand Prix racing

Two outdoor attractions offer miniature golf and stock car racing

Play miniature golf on the two 9-hole courses featuring a fantasy atmosphere. Combine this with bumper boats, video games, batting cages, and sprint cars for a great afternoon or evening of fun.

Next door, race three sizes of racecars along the mile track. The Virage is a ¾ scale formula race-car. The Grand Virage, the larger car, seats two. The third car, the Mini Virage allows kids 8 years of age or 54 inches or taller to experience the fun.

Hours

Closed Mondays & Tuesdays in the winter

Mon. – Thurs.	11 am - 11 pm
Friday	Noon - Midnight
Saturday	11 am – 1 am
Sunday	Noon – 11 pm

Cost - *Miniature golf*

Adults	$5.95
Children under 13	$4.95
Children under	Free

Grand Prix Racing
Prices vary according to car

Directions

From downtown take I-10 West to the Callaghen exit and go right on Callaghen, turn right on Pine Brook, then a right on Briaridge Drive. Turn left on Cherry Ridge.

125

RETAMA PARK

One Retama Parkway, Selma 78154
210-651-7000

Visit one of San Antonio's newest attractions

Monitors make horse racing more entertaining. With a world-class track, the park features year-round horse racing, live or simulcast from other tracks throughout the country. Enjoy the races from the second floor grandstand, from the fourth floor air-conditioned clubhouse, or from ground level. Televised races provide opportunities to wager on horses anywhere in the United States. Retama Park offers easy viewing from hundreds of monitors throughout the facility.

The wagering program comes with simple instructions, making it easy for beginners. Also available in Spanish. Call and ask about group rates for 20 people or more.

Suit the occasion with dining at a fine restaurant overlooking the tracks or eating the usual chili cheese dogs and tacos at the fast food court.

Hours - Times vary, call for the schedule

Cost

General Admission (live racing)	$2.50
Clubhouse Admission	$3.50
Simulcast Admission	$1
Children under 15 (with adult)	Free
Seniors over 62:	
General Admission	$1.50
Clubhouse Admission	$2.50
Parking	$2

Directions

15 minutes north of downtown San Antonio. Take I-35 and exit 174-A, north of Loop 1604.

RIPLEY'S BELIEVE IT OR NOT PLAZA THEATRE OF WAX

301 Alamo Plaza, San Antonio
210-224-9299

See the unbelievable

You'll find two attractions at the same location. See them both and get a discount. Based on the original television series and the travels of the famous cartoonist, Ripley's Believe It or Not exhibits the strange and exotic from around the world. With 8 different galleries and over 500 exhibits, the attraction includes a man with double pupils in each eye, a hand-written Bible, a beautiful 5-foot papier-mâché Madonna, and the world's tallest man. Experience the hurricane simulator, with winds over a 55 mph.

The Plaza Theatre of Wax features over 250 life-size figures. Look for Kevin Costner, Denzel Washington, Jim Carrey, Whoopie Goldberg, Brad Pitt, Julia Roberts, and Captain Picard. Bring the camera; you'll enjoy posing with the stars. The theatre divides into themes of Hollywood, Horror, History, and Religion. The box office closes 1 hour before closing time.

Hours
Winter (Closed Christmas Day)

Sun. – Thurs.	9 am – 7 pm
Fri. – Sat.	9 am – 10 pm

Summer

Daily	9 am – 10 pm

Cost(combo ticket)

Adults	$14.95
Children (4 – 12)	$7.95
Seniors	$13.95

Directions - Across from the Alamo

SCOBEE PLANETARIUM
at San Antonio College

1300 San Pedro Avenue
San Antonio
210-733-2910

See a planetarium show,
then visit the observatory

Enjoy trekking through the solar system or gazing at the night's sky constellations every Friday night. Attendees of the evening's last performance get an additional treat. Weather permitting, they can stay for more at the observatory.

Shows last approximately one hour and allow children as young as 6 years of age. Wear comfortable casual clothing.

Offering shows for kids, the planetarium includes children ages 4 and older. Shows make popular field trips for school groups. Call for more details. Please note that the planetarium closes mid-July through August each year.

Hours

Fridays . . . . 6 pm – 9 pm

Cost

Free

Directions

North of downtown. From I-35N exit San Pedro Avenue and go north (left). Will be past E. Park Street.

SPLASHTOWN

3600 I-35 North
San Antonio 78219
210-227-1400

Have a fun day at this water park

Want to save a bundle? Remember to bring an empty can or some other proof of purchase from any Country Time Lemonade product and receive half-off admission before 5 pm. One can will include half-off admission for up to six adults and children.

Besides offering a great bargain, the water park offers something fun for everyone: body slides, tube rides, a wave pool, and the popular Kids' Kove. You'll find the Lone Star Luge, a huge slide with twists and turns, a hit with the family.

Bring a cooler of food for the picnic area adjacent the park. Life jackets and tubes come with the admission price. The park offers rental lockers and a concession stand. Watch for special events and concerts. Parking is free.

Hours

Sun. – Thurs.	11 am – 9 pm
Fri. and Sat.	11 am – 10 pm

Cost

Adults	$19.99
Children under 4 feet	$14.95
Children under age 2	Free
Seniors 65+	Free

Directions

North of downtown San Antonio on I-35 North. Take the Splashtown Road exit #160. Will be on the right.

TEXAS TROLLEY HOP

216 Alamo Plaza, San Antonio
210-225-8587 Information
210-212-5395 Group Reservations

A fun and convenient way to see San Antonio

The Texas Trolley offers two 60-minute tours aboard their air-conditioned and heated trolleys. Choose either the Historic Tour or the Uptown Tour. If that's a difficult decision, they offer both at a discount. Better yet, for a few dollars more, the Hop Pass gives you unlimited reboarding privileges at any of the Texas Trolley Hop Stops. Spend the day sightseeing at the places that interest you.

The Historic Tour includes the Alamo, the IMAX Theatre, the River Walk, HemisFair Park, Mission San Jose and Mission Concepcion, the Lone Star Buckhorn Museums, Market Square, San Fernando Cathedral, and La Villita.

On the Uptown Tour, you will see Ft. Sam Houston, the San Antonio Botanical Gardens, the McNay Art Museum, Olmos Park, the San Antonio Zoo, Brackenridge Park, the Witte Museum, and the San Antonio Museum of Art.

Daily Hours .... 9:30 am
60-Minute Historic Tour or 60-Minute Uptown Tour Costs
Adults $9.95
Children 3-11 .... $4.95
Adults (with Hop Pass) $11.95
Children (with Hop Pass) $5.95
One-day Combination Costs—includes Hop Pass
Adults $16.95
Children 3-11 .... $8.95
Two-day Combination Costs—includes Hop Pass for two days
Adults $19.95
Children 3-11 .... $9.95

Directions - Board trolley at the Alamo Visitor Center at the Menger Hotel next to the Alamo.

VIA SAN ANTONIO STREETCARS
(VIA Metropolitan Transit)

112 N. Soledad (downtown office), San Antonio
210-362-2000
210-362-2020 Customer information

800 W. Myrtle, San Antonio
210-227-5371

Crossroads Park-and-Ride
In the Crossroads Mall Parking Lot
210-735-3317

Check out San Antonio's streetcar system

Cheap and easy. Anyone looking for a convenient way to get around San Antonio will enjoy the streetcar system. Not only is it the best way to get around downtown, fares cost only 75 cents. Routes circulate popular tourist destinations, shopping centers, and city parks. Enjoy riding the open-air, rubber-tired replicas of the turn-of-the-century trolleys that operated in San Antonio 50 years ago.

Streetcars operate from early morning until late in the evening. Wait at a stop no longer than about 10 minutes. Pay with cash, streetcar tokens, or ride all you want for the day for $5 with a Streetcar Pass.

Schedules and route information can easily be obtained at one of their offices or at the Alamo Visitor Center across from the Alamo.

VIA Transit System offers schoolchildren opportunities for field trips by way of their bus system called VIA's Class Pass. Call for more information, 210-362-2370. The program provides a trip planning guide and a list of popular field trips in the city area.

Locations

1. Acadiana Cafe
2. Alamo Cafe
3. Apple Annie's Tea Room & Bakery
4. Boudro's, A Texas Bistro on the River Walk
5. Carranza's
6. Chris Madrid's Nachos and Burgers
7. Dick's Last Resort
8. El Mirador Restaurant
9. Golden Wok Chinese Restaurant
10. Guenther House Restaurant
11. Grey Moss Inn
12. La Fogata
13. Liberty Bar
14. Magic Time Machine
15. Mi Tierra Cafe and Bakery
16. Old San Francisco Steak House
17. Paloma Blanca
18. Rio Rio Cantina
19. Rosario's Mexican Cafe Y Cantina
20. Rudy's Country Store and BBQ
21. Schilo's Delicatessen
22. Sea Island Shrimp House
23. Tower of the Americas Restaurant
24. Zuni Grill

Chapter 7
WHERE TO EAT?

ACADIANA CAFE

1289 Southwest Loop 410
San Antonio
210-674-0019

Cajun

This popular Cajun restaurant proves that not all the spicy food in San Antonio is Tex-Mex. Parents needn't worry though. There's plenty here to keep all ages happy.

Mouth-watering, buttery biscuits served with honey will have kids and adults begging for more. Fried catfish and crispy hush puppies are top-notch.

During the holidays, call ahead and see if it's one of the days that Acadiana is serving its famous deep-fried turkey. Whole turkeys also are available year-round. (advance ordering required).

Hours

Sun.-Thur. .... 11 am-10 pm
Fri. and Sat. .... 11 am-11 pm

Cost

$6 -15

Directions

From downtown, take 410 West, exit #8 (Lakeside Parkway). Continue on the access road. Will be at the West Lakes Theater's parking lot.

ALAMO CAFE

10060 I-10 West, San Antonio 78230
210-691-8827
and
14250 Highway 281 North, San Antonio 78232
210-495-2233

Mexican

Even if these restaurants weren't so well placed (one in the airport vicinity, the other near Six Flags Fiesta Texas), they'd be worth the drive. Alamo Café knows how to keep the chips, salsa, and warm tortillas coming and the beverages (including soft drinks) constantly refilled.

Best bets include an incomparable tortilla soup and chicken fajita combo. Kids go for their mild but tasty version of chile con queso. Chicken fried steak is oversized and the perfect contrast between crispy breading and tender interior. Save room for their famous margarita pie. No reservations.

Hours

Sun. - Thurs. . . . . 10:45 am - 11 pm
Fri. - Sat. . . . . 10:45 am - Midnight

Cost - $4 -8

Directions

For the restaurant at 10060 I-10, take I-10 West to the Huebner exit (outside Loop 410) and take the turnaround to cross back over I-10. The restaurant will be approximately .5 mile on the right on the access road.

For the restaurant at 14250 Highway 281 North, take Highway 281 North to the Winding Way/Oak Shadows exit (outside Loop 410). The restaurant will be approximately .25 mile on the right side of the access road.

APPLE ANNIE'S TEA ROOM & BAKERY

555 W. Bitters Road
San Antonio
210-491-0226

American

Located in the midst of Artisan's Alley, a delightful mix of some 20 quaint shops (kids will love The Stamping Factory). This tearoom has as its motto, "You can't leave hungry."

A savory cheese appetizer greets guests as they're seated. From there, pick between homemade soups, savory salads and sandwiches, and daily specials such as King Ranch chicken. Sinfully rich desserts, including the tearoom's signature Sawdust Pie and Apple Crunch Cake, are the perfect ending. Open daily for lunch until 2:30 pm (3 pm on the weekend) and for desserts until 5:30 pm.

Hours

Mon. – Fri.	11 am – 2:30 pm
Sat. – Sun.	11 am – 3 pm

Cost
$5 - $8

Directions

Take 281 North to Bitters Road and go left one mile. Will be on the right.

Where To Eat?

BOUDRO'S, A TEXAS BISTRO ON THE RIVER WALK

421 E. Commerce
San Antonio
210-224-8484

Southwestern

Considered the star in the crown that is San Antonio's river dining, Boudro's is the perfect place to leisurely watch River Walk crowds while you dine in casual comfort.

Order guacamole and get ready for the kids to be fascinated as it's prepared tableside. Who knows? With that kind of incentive, they may even take to the kitchen when they get home.

Hours

Sun. - Thurs. . . . . 11 am - 11 pm
Fri. - Sat. . . . . 11 am - Midnight

Cost

$12 - $20

Directions

Located in the middle of the River Walk, between the Hyatt Regency and the Hilton Palacio Del Rio.

CARRANZA'S

701 Austin St.
San Antonio
210-223-0903

Barbecue/Italian/Mexican/Seafood

Family can't settle on whether to eat seafood, Italian, Mexican, or barbecue? Carranza's lets you have all of the above, and then some.

Located in a charmingly restored stone building near downtown, Carranza's began serving barbecue out of a tiny grocery store and grew from there. Seafood entrees—particularly sea cakes served with dual sauces—are incomparable. Kids will love their spaghetti and meatballs. An outpost at 2908 N. St. Mary's St. (210-735-6801) serves barbecue only.

Hours

(Closed Sunday)
Lunch
Mon. – Fri. . . . . 11 am – 2 pm
Dinner
Mon. – Thur. . . . . 5 pm – 10 pm
Fri, and Sat. . . . . 5 pm – 11 pm

Cost

$6 – $28.50

Directions

From downtown, take Broadway north to Jones and go right. Cross Alamo and go left on Austin. Will be on the left, look for the 1st old limestone building (Carranza's Grocery and Market).

Where To Eat?

CHRIS MADRID'S NACHOS AND BURGERS

1900 Blanco Road
San Antonio
210-735-3552

Burgers/Mexican

Burgers and nachos—need we say more? Only that these are some of the juiciest, floppiest, tastiest burgers you'll ever see, including the beanburger loaded with refried beans, cheese, and crunchy Fritos. Macho Nachos are as loaded as you can get and deliciously messy and satisfying.

Hours

(Closed Sunday)
Mon. – Sat. . . . . 11 am – 10 pm

Cost

$3.50 - $6

Directions

From downtown, take San Pedro Street north to Hildebrand. Go left and continue to Blanco and go left again. Will be on Blanco and Hollywood Streets.

DICK'S LAST RESORT ON THE RIVER WALK

406 Navarro
San Antonio 78205
210-224-0026

American/Seafood

Dick's on the River Walk is family fun during the day, but more adult oriented at night (no kids or teens are allowed after 9 pm, so plan accordingly). You'll get lots of good-natured ribbing as you snack on catfish, shrimp, and steak. A wide assortment of kids' plates offer everything from burgers to corn dogs and ribs.

Hours

Daily .... 11 am – 2 pm

Cost

Lunch $4-6
Dinner $10-18

Directions

Located on the River Walk under the Navarro Bridge, across from Planet Hollywood.

Where To Eat?

EL MIRADOR RESTAURANT

722 S. St. Mary's
San Antonio 78205
210-225-9444

Mexican

One of San Antonio's most beloved restaurants, El Mirador is everything you'd want in an established Tex-Mex restaurant—modestly priced, delicious food in a comfortable atmosphere. Soups, including Caldo Xochitl, are El Mirador's specialty, but puffy tacos, enchiladas, and chalupas compuestas are just as memorable. Prices and menu offerings are slightly more upscale at dinner.

Hours

Sunday . . . . 9 am – 3 pm
Breakfast
Mon. – Sat. . . . . 6:30 am – 9 am
Lunch
Mon. – Sat. . . . . 11 am – 3 pm
Dinner
Tues. – Thurs. . . . . 6:30 pm – 9 pm
Fri. and Sat. . . . . 6:30 pm – 10 pm

Cost

Lunch . . . . $3.95 - $7
Dinner . . . . $5.95 - $17

Directions

On the corner of S. St. Mary's
and Durango Streets.

GOLDEN WOK CHINESE RESTAURANT

8822 Wurzbach Road
San Antonio
210-615-8282

Chinese

If your kids have never had dim sum, this is the place to take them. On Saturdays and Sundays from 11:30 a.m.-1:30 p.m., carts piled high with steamer trays are rolled around the restaurant. When they stop at your table, you pick and choose at will from such items as shrimp dumplings and sweet rice tied in banana leaves. The earlier you come, the better the selection—some 20-25 items most days.

Hours

Mon. – Sat. .... 11 am – 10 pm

Cost

$5.95 - $2

Directions

From downtown, take I-10 West and exit Wurzbach. Go left. Will be 3 or 4 blocks down on the left.

GREY MOSS INN

19010 Scenic Loop Road
San Antonio
210-695-8301

Steaks

For 63 years, the Grey Moss Inn has been serving its famous steaks (cooked over a well in the courtyard) in a Hill Country setting that originally was a getaway from the heat of the city. The drive there is romantic—albeit dark and a bit winding.

Jalapeno- and bacon-stuffed twice-baked potatoes are tops, as is the signature squash casserole, served at the restaurant since it opened. Kids will be fascinated by the candles that flicker at the tables. With their waxy build-up, the candles look like they've been burning since the restaurant's opening in the '20s.

Hours

Mon. – Sat. . . . . 5 pm – 10 pm

Cost

$20 - $45

Directions

From downtown, take I-10 West to 1604 and go west. Exit Babcock and go right for 6 miles, until it deadends. Go left on Scenic Loop Road and travel 2.5 miles. Will be on the left.

GUENTHER HOUSE RESTAURANT

205 E. Guenther
San Antonio 78204
210-227-1061

American

Located in the King William area and part of the century-old Pioneer Flour Mill, Guenther House is the perfect place to enjoy a leisurely breakfast away from the rush of downtown.

Towering waffles are an excellent choice, as are the breakfast tacos and any of the fresh-baked goods.

Be sure to visit the accompanying store where you can purchase top-quality foodstuffs to recreate your own Guenther House specialties at home.

Hours

Mon. – Sat. .... 7 am – 3 pm
Sunday .... 8 am – 2 pm

Cost

$2.25- $6.95

Directions

Located next to the King William District. Take S. Alamo south of downtown and go right on E. Guenther.

LA FOGATA

2427 Vance Jackson
San Antonio 78213
210-340-1337

Mexican

For 20 years, La Fogata has set the standard for Mexican dining in San Antonio. Eat outdoors in one of the city's loveliest alfresco settings or inside in cool comfort. Rajas con crema and quesadillas de hongos stuffed with white Mexican cheese and mushrooms are blissful, as are the green enchiladas.

The smoky, roasted salsa is available for take-home. Trust us—you'll want to.

Hours

Sat. and Sun Breakfast. . . . . 8 am – 11 am
Mon. – Thur. . . . . 11 am – 10 pm
Friday . . . . 11 am –11 pm
Saturday . . . . 11 am – 11 pm
Sunday . . . . 11 am – 10 pm

Cost

$5.75 - $19.95

Directions

From downtown, take I-10 West and exit Vance Jackson. Go right. Will be on the left approximately 1 mile down.

Where To Eat?

LIBERTY BAR

328 E. Josephine St.
San Antonio 78215
210-227-1187

American

Don't be frightened, but this building tilts noticeably to the east. Not to fear, however—San Antonians have been safely dining there for years.

The eclectic, slightly upscale, somewhat Southern menu has something to please nearly everyone. Mexican-inspired entrees are especially satisfying, as is the restaurant's famous decadent chocolate cake.

Hours

Mon. – Thur. . . . . 11:30 am – 10:30 pm
Fri. – Sat. . . . . 11:30 am – Midnight
Sunday . . . . 10:30 am – 10:30 pm

Cost

$6.75 – $18.95

Directions

From downtown, take 281 North and exit Josephine. Will be on the corner. Or take Braodway north of downtown and go left on Josephine. Will be on the left.

Where To Eat?

MAGIC TIME MACHINE

902 Northeast Loop 410
San Antonio
210-828-1470

Steaks

As much entertainment as restaurant, Magic Time Machine entertains the young and the young at heart. A crazy cast of costumed characters serve your meals and create a magical mood with their jokes, songs, and friendly banter.

Kids will love the real '53 MG roadster that's been gutted and serves as a soup and salad bar. Parents will enjoy the fact that someone is giving them a break and doing some of the entertaining.

Hours

Sun. – Thurs. . . . . 5:30 pm – 10 pm
Fril – Sun. . . . . 5 pm –10:30 pm

Cost

$10 - $22

Directions

From downtown, take 281 North. Go east on 410 and exit Broadway. Pass Broadway. Will be on the right.

MI TIERRA CAFE AND BAKERY

218 Produce Row (in El Mercado)
San Antonio
210-225-1262

Mexican

Twenty-four hours a day, 365 days a year, Mi Tierra turns out its Mexican specialties. We find it most satisfying late at night, when other restaurants have long since closed their doors.

Caldo del Mercado is popular, as are the chiles rellenos and chalupas. But for sheer gluttony, try the Special Mexican Dinner—taco, tamale, cheese enchilada, chile con queso, guacamole, rice, beans, and flour tortillas.

An accompanying bakery counter sells fresh Mexican breads, cookies, and candies.

Hours

24 hours, year-round

Cost

$5 - $16

Directions

Located in Market Square, at I-35 and Commerce.

OLD SAN FRANCISCO STEAKHOUSE

10223 Sahara
San Antonio
210-342-2321

Steaks/Seafood

When you make reservations at this Gay '90s theme restaurant, request "The Swing Room" where the girl on the red velvet swing pumps herself to dizzying heights, ultimately ringing a bell on the 30-foot ceiling with her foot. Kids are allowed to take a (much-tamer) swing ride.

Diners start their meal with an oversized block of Swiss cheese and fresh-baked bread. Prime rib is good, as is the fish and chicken. A separate children's menu with prices starting at $3.50 is available.

Hours

Mon. – Thurs.	5 pm – 10 pm
Fri. – Sat.	5 pm – 11 pm
Sunday	4 pm – 11 pm

Cost

$16.95 - $36

Directions

Located 15 minutes from downtown. Take 281 North to the 410 Loop and go west. Exit San Pedro and travel north approximately 1 mile to Sahara. Go right. Will be on the right.

PALOMA BLANCA

5148 Broadway
San Antonio
210-822-6151

Mexican

One of San Antonio's newest, Paloma Blanca offers a memorable taste experience at modest prices.

Two varieties of salsa are among the best in the city, as are the homemade corn and flour tortillas. Order the soup, enchiladas, or chicken specialties with confidence. Homemade *tres leches* cake (soaked with three milks for an almost cheesecake-like consistency) is legendary.

Hours

Sun. – Tues.	11 am – 9 pm
Wed. – Thurs.	11 am – 10 pm
Fri. – Sat.	11 am – 10:30 pm
Saturday (breakfast)	8 am – 11 am

Cost

$5.25 – $10.95

Directions

Take Broadway north of downtown. Will be 3 stop signs past Hildebrand on the right.

RIO RIO CANTINA ON THE RIVER WALK

421 E. Commerce
San Antonio 78205
210-226-8462

Mexican

Located one level up from the river, Rio Rio offers a lush view of River Walk activity in a cool, comfy atmosphere. Portions are oversized, so order carefully.

Rio Rio Enchiladas are a good pick, as are the appetizer quesadillas, which are more than enough for a kid's meal for sharing. Salsa is top-notch and free-flowing.

Hours

Daily .... 11 am – 10 pm to 10:30 pm

Cost

$6.95 – $13.95

Directions

On the Riverwalk. On the corner of Losoya and Commerce Streets.

ROSARIO'S MEXICAN CAFE Y CANTINA

1014 S. Alamo
San Antonio, TX 78210
(210) 223-1806

Tex Mex

San Antonio's trendiest new Tex-Mex restaurant is just a few minutes from the heart of downtown San Antonio. It can get a little crowded at night, so lunch is a great time to make a family visit. On the other hand, the dinner noise is usually enough to keep most kids on good behavior and a child on less-than-stellar behavior seldom bothers other diners. A bright, colorful ambience sets the stage for top-notch salsa, chips and a wide assortment of Mexican specialties.

Hours

Mon. . . . . 11 am – 3 pm
Tues.-Thurs. . . . . 11 am – 10 pm
Fri.-Sat. . . . . 11 am – 11 pm

Cost

$4-$10

Directions

Less than 5 minutes from downtown on South Alamo.

RUDY'S COUNTRY STORE AND BBQ

24152 I-10 West
Leon Springs 78257
210-698-2141
and
10623 Westover Hills Blvd.
San Antonio
210-520-5552

Barbecue

You'll find lots of kid-pleasing food at either of these two locations (Leon Springs is the original), but there's plenty to make adults happy, too, including mouth-watering pork ribs, tenderloin, and brisket.

Grab a soft drink from icy troughs, then prepare to stand in line a while, as these are popular places. Regulars know to order some of Rudy's creamed corn on the side and to grab an extra bottle or two of barbecue sauce to take home with them.

Hours

Sun. – Thur. . . . . 10 am – 10 pm
Fri.- Sat. . . . . 10 am – 11 pm

Cost

$2 - $10.95

Directions

For the restaurant in Leon Springs coming from downtown, take I-10 West and exit 551 (Leon Springs). Will be on the right on the access road.

The San Antonio retaurant is located at 151 (Raymond Stotzer Freeway) and Westover Hills, across the street from the entrance to Sea World.

SCHILO'S DELICATESSEN

428 E. Commerce
San Antonio 78205
210-223-6692

Delicatessen

For 80-plus years, this downtown institution (near the River Walk, one level up) has been producing such specialties as split pea soup, chicken and dumplings and deli sandwiches. But it's their homemade root-beer served in frosty mugs that is most noteworthy. You'll never want to go back to the bottled kind after you taste the real stuff. (One free refill is included in the price—you'll want to take it.)

Hours

Mon. – Sat. . . . . 7 am – 8:30 pm

Cost

$5 - $9

Directions

Downtown at E. Commerce near the River Walk, between Presa and Navarro Streets.

SEA ISLAND SHRIMP HOUSE

5959 Northwest Loop 410, San Antonio 78238
210-520-3033

322 W. Rector, San Antonio
210-342-7771

4323 Amerisuites Dr., San Antonio 78230
210-558-8989

Seafood

So busy are these restaurants during rush hours that you get two numbers—one for a table, then one for your order. Not to worry. The system works well at this casual restaurant, waits are short, and the reasonably priced food is worth it.

Fried shrimp and fish are stellar. Cole slaw and hush puppies accompany beautifully. Gumbo is a must-have.

Hours

Mon. – Sat. . . . . 10:45 am – 9 pm
Sunday . . . . 11 am – 8 pm

Cost
$6 - $12

Directions from downtown

For Northwest Loop 410, take 281 North to 410 West and exit Exchange Parkway. Will be .5 mile on the right.

For Rector, take 281 North to 410 West and exit San Pedro Ave., go south. Turn left on W. Rector. On the immediate right behind the mall.

For Amerisuites, take I-10 W, exit Huebner Road. Stay on the access road. On your right before Huebner.

TOWER OF THE AMERICAS

222 HemisFair Park
San Antonio 78205
210-223-3101

American

This revolving restaurant atop the Tower of the Americas was part of HemisFair '68. Thirty years later, it's still revolving (one revolution per hour) and serving customers a spectacular view of all parts of the city.

Steak and seafood top the list. Kids have their own reasonably priced menu with their choice of nachos, fried shrimp, chicken fingers, and burgers.

Hours

Lunch

Mon. – Fri. . . . . 11 am – 2 pm
Sat. – Sun. . . . . 11 am – 2:30 pm

Dinner

Sun. – Thur. . . . . 5:30 pm – 10 pm
Fri. – Sun. . . . . 5:30 pm – 10:30 pm

Cost

$12 - $30

Directions

Located downtown on Bowie, between Market and Durango Streets.

ZUNI GRILL

511 River Walk
210-227-0864

American

Besides good food, Zuni Grill has another way of making parents happy. When you come in late in the evening with small kids that are getting tired and grumpy, Zuni's waitstaff often will bring complimentary bowls of chopped fruit or flour tortillas for snacking along with the more adult chips and salsa. Anything to please is their motto. Adults will especially appreciate this gesture.

Hours

Daily . . . . 8 am – 10 pm

Cost

$9.95- $20

Directions

At Losoya and Crocket. On the River Walk, two restaurants from the Hyatt Regency.

Locations

1. Antique Center
2. Center for Antiques
3. Dagen Bela Ortiz Galeria
4. Gallery of the Southwest
5. Guadalupe Cultural Arts Gallery
6. Booksmiths of San Antonio
7. Cheever Books
8. The Twig Bookshop
9. Central Market
10. Whole Foods Market
11. Bussey's Flea Market
12. Eisenhauer Road Flea Market
13. Flea Market
14. San Marcos Factory Stores
15. SAS Factory Shoe Store
16. Tanger Outlet Center
17. Alamo Heights
18. Market Square
19. La Villita Historic District
20. Alamo Quarry Market
21. Kallison's Western Wear
22. Lucchese Boots
23. Paris Hatter

Chapter 8
UNIQUE PLACES TO SHOP

ANTIQUE SHOPS

Antique Center
11345 West Ave.
San Antonio 78213
210-344-4131

Find a little of everything at this antique center, one of the largest antique stores away from the downtown area. Specialty items include juke boxes, Coca-Cola machines, glass, and signs. Go left two blocks from Blanco Road on West Street.

Mon. – Sat.	10am – 6pm
Sun.	noon – 5pm

Center for Antiques
8505 Broadway (outside Loop 410)
San Antonio 78217
210-804-6300

Over 115 dealers fill this center with every kind of antique imaginable. One of the largest antique dealers in San Antonio.

Mon. – Fri.	10 am – 6pm
Sat.	10 am – 6pm
Sun.	noon – 5pm

ART GALLERIES

The Dagen Bela Ortiz Galeria
102 Concho (Market Square)
San Antonio 78207
210-225-0731

Shop at one of the most unique galleries in San Antonio, featuring works of local Hispanic artists and artists from Mexico. The gallery displays custom jewelry, pottery, bronze sculptures, Mexican folk art, and other fascinating art pieces.

Weekdays . . . . 10 am – 5:30 pm
Weekends . . . . open until 8 pm

Gallery of the Southwest
13485 Blanco (and Bitters Roads)
San Antonio 78231
210-493-3344

Every things in this store is Southwestern. Shop for items from the Hopi, Navaho, and Zuni Indians: rugs, pottery, paintings, watercolors, and oils. The shop offers collectibles and interesting pawn pieces.

Tues. – Sat. . . . . 10 am – 5pm

Guadalupe Cultural Arts Center Gallery
325 S. Salado Street
San Antonio 78207
210-271-0379

Dedicated to the arts and culture of the Chicano, Latino, and Native American people.

Mon.–Fri. . . . . 10 am - 6 pm

THE SHOPS IN BOERNE

If you like antique shops, take a drive to Boerne, just 25 minutes north of San Antonio. Here you will find lots of antique and specialty shops clustered along Main Street. Boerne has over 30 little antique shops. Shops you want to browsing through are **Buy, Buy Birdie** (438 S. Main St.), **Heyday** (615 S. Main St.), and **The Christmas Shoppe** (132 S. Main St.). Heyday specializes in Mexican antique furniture and, for those of you who can't get enough of it, folk art.

The **Boerne Market Days** happens the 2nd weekend of each month. Catering to families, activities include a festive-like atmosphere with arts and craft booths, antiques, collectibles, and more. This takes place on the Main Plaza in downtown.

Twice a year, Boerne explodes with antique dealers: **The Hill Country Antique Show**, the 1st weekend in March, and the **Boerne Antique Show** in October, one weekend in October, 830-249-8000. Antique-lovers highly regard these shows. Shoppers find folk art, quilts, books, pewter, glassware, dried florals, antique postcards, jewelry and much more. Admission charged.

While you're in Boerne, you must try the breakfast tacos at **Mague's** (934 N. Main St.). And then there's **Bumdoodlers** (929 N. Main St.) for lunch. Maybe its dive-like atmosphere will appeal to your teens, but the homemade bread will be a hit with everyone else. Tasty sandwiches are their specialty; but the soups, salads, pies, and cheesecake are good too.

Bear Moon Bakery, serves thousands of their popular kolaches to hungry tourists and locals each month. One of their tasty Texas-sized, fresh-baked cinnamon rolls will just about feed a family. Of course, choosing from any of their pastries will be a tough decision.

Oh, and one more place I like to mention is the **Peach Tree Kountry Kitchen** (448 S. Main St.). Eat inside a restored Victorian house. Their home-style menu changed every day, but you won't forget the cheese rolls. This little eatery is big on Hill Country charm.

BOOKSTORES

Booksmiths of San Antonio
209 Alamo Plaza
San Antonio 78205
210-271-9177

This family-owned store specializes in regional books—from southwestern cookbooks to books on the Alamo. Downstairs you'll find literature for kids. Stop at their deli for tasty pastries, soups, and sandwiches. Located across from the Alamo.

Cheever Books
140 Carnahan St.
San Antonio 78209
210-824-2665

Located in the Alamo Heights area across from the Witte Museum, this bookstore carries a huge selection of used books—many rare. Take Broadway past 35N (near Brachenridge Park) to Carnahan St. and go right.

Mon.-Sat. . . . . 10 am – 8 pm
Sun. . . . . noon – 8 pm

Twig Bookshop
5005 Broadway
Alamo Heights 78209
800-729-8944 • 210-826-6411

Located in the delightful Alamo Heights area minutes from downtown San Antonio, the Twig Bookshop carries a nice selection of children's literature, fiction, and Texana.

FOOD MARKETS

Central Market
4821 Broadway (at Hildebrand)
Alamo Heights 78209
210-368-8600

See what's in store at H.E.B.'s grandest 2-story grocery market, featuring over 4000 specialty items. Chefs prepare 80 different dishes ready for you to take home. You'll find natural foods, fresh seafood, a made-from-scratch bakery, a huge floral department, a catering service, a gift gallery, a cooking school, and much more.

Opens daily . . . . 7 am – 10 pm

Whole Foods Market
255 E. Basse Road
San Antonio 78209
210-826-4676

A national chain store, Whole Foods Market sells a large variety of baked goodies, nuts, grains, granolas, cheeses, and other health food products. What's most popular is their deli counter. The store offers many kinds of specialty sandwiches and prepared dishes.

Opens daily . . . . 9 am–10 pm

FLEA MARKETS

Bussey's Flea Market
18738 I-35 North
SanAntonio
210-651-6830

Opens Saturdays and Sundays 7 am – 5:30 pm, with 20 acres of indoor and outdoor vendors. Rent a booth or come to browse.You'll find everything imaginable, from antiques, tools, and crafts, to garage sale and import items. Located about 30 minutes from downtown.Worth the drive.

Eisenhauer Road Flea Market
3903 Eisenhauer Road
SanAntonio 78218
210-653-7592

An indoor air-conditioned market that features all kinds of items, used and new.Also offers barbecue food and snack bars.Take Broadway north of downtown and continue to the right (northeast) from Austin Parkway.Turn right on Eisenhauer.

OpensWed.– Fri. . . . . noon – 7pm
Sat. – Sun. . . . . 9am – 7pm

Flea Market
12280 Highway 16 South (1 mile south of Loop 410)
SanAntonio
210-624-2666

A huge authentic Mexican market filled with all kinds of things: clothes, crafts, fruits, vegetables, and foods like homemade tamales and tortillas. Festive atmosphere with live music.

Sat. and Sun. . . . . 10 am – 6 pm

OUTLET STORES

San Marcos Factory Stores

3939 I-35 South (Exit 200), San Marcos 78666
800-628-9465 • 512-396-7183

Take 25-75% off at the largest factory outlet in Texas, with over 119 stores. Many upscale name brands stores, such as Donna Karan, Polo Ralph Lauren, and Ann Taylor. Just 45 min. from San Antonio.

Mon. – Sat. . . . . 10 am – 9 pm
Sun. . . . . 11 am – 6 pm

SAS Factory Shoe Store

101 New Laredo Highway (at Zaramore)
San Antonio 78207
210-924-6507

San Antonio manufactured leather shoes with small, hardly-noticeable defects at great savings. Save $20-30 on a pair of shoes. Buy shoes for the whole family— infants to adults—along with purses and belts.

Mon. – Fri. . . . . 9 am – 6 pm
Sat. . . . . 9 am – 5 pm

Tanger Outlet Center

4015 I-35 South (Exit 200), San Marcos 78666
800-408-8424

Across the street from the San Marcos Factory Stores, shop at one of the largest Tanger Outlet Centers. Over 50 stores with popular name brands such as Reebok, Disney, Dansk, Liz Claiborne, Claiborne for Men, Elizabeth, Kitchen Collection, Polo Jean Co. and much more. You'll find yourself in shopper's heaven.

Mon. – Sat. . . . . 9 am – 9 pm
Sun. . . . . 11 am – 6 pm

UNIQUE PLACES TO SHOP

Alamo Heights

Broadway, San Antonio

This upscale suburban area, with its array of classy shops along Broadway, makes for a fun afternoon. Two small interesting shopping areas include the Lincoln Heights (Broadway and Basse) and The Collection (Broadway and Sunset). Shop hours vary.

Alamo Quarry Market

Hwy 281 North (at E. Basse Road), San Antonio

It's the giant smokestacks in the center of the complex—one of San Antonio's oldest landmarks—that catches your attention. Shop at this unique Post-Industrial designed shopping center that now fills the old rock-crushing Alamo Cement Plant. Shops include Borders Books, Canyon Café, Joe's Crab Shack, Paesano's, Whole Foods Market, and more.

La Villita Historic District

418 Villita Street, San Antonio • 210-207-8610

What was the first original settlement is now a hot spot for art galleries. You'll find unique little shops. Buy tickets here for the Arneson Theater or attend one of Fiesta's biggest events, *A Night in Old San Antonio* in April.

Open daily . . . . 10 am – 5 pm

Market Square

514 W. Commerce Street, San Antonio 78207
210-207-8600

Any tourist wanting to see San Antonio must visit Market Square. Eat great Tex-Mex food, listen to mariachis, and shop at authentic shops. Festivals frequently take place in the open plazas.

Open daily 10 am to 5 pm (summer to 8 pm)

UNIQUE SHOPS

Kallison's Western Wear

123 S. Flores St. (at Dolorosa St.)
San Antonio 78204
210-222-1364

Kallison is the place for western wear—San Antonio's oldest. Shop here for hats, shirts, jeans, boots.
Open Mon. – Sat. . . . . 10 am – 6 pm.

Lucchese Boots

4025 Broadway (south of Hildebrand)
San Antonio 78209
210-828-9419

An immigrant from Italy, Sam Lucchese, brought to San Antonio the boot-making skills that produced the best in western boots. Now a corporation, see some of the finest boots, many from exotic hides.
Open daily . . . . 10 am – 6 pm

Paris Hatter

119 Broadway (downtown)
San Antonio 78205
210-223-3453

One of the most unique shops to San Antonio, the Paris Hatter has custom fitted western hats for nearly a century to many a well-known celebrity. One of the largest western hat stores in the country.
Open daily . . . . .9 am – 6 pm

1. Annual River Walk Mud Festival
2. Cowboy Breakfast
3. San Antonio CineFestival
4. San Antonio Stock Show and Rodeo
5. Dyeing O' the River Green Parade
6. Fiesta San Antonio
7. Annual Tejano Conjunto Festival
8. Cinco DeMayo Celebration
9. The Return of the Chili Queens
10. Concert Under the Stars
11. Shakespears in the Park
12. Texas Folklife Festival
13. Contemporary Art Month
14. Annual Jazz'S Alive
15. Big Country River Featival
16. Fiestas Patria
17. Inter-American Bookfair & Festival
18. International Theatre Festival
19. Oktoberfest at San Antonio
20. Feria de Santa Cecilia and Fiestas
21. Lighting Ceremony and River Walk Holiday
22. Fiesta de las Luminarias
23. Las Posadas
24. Rivercenter Christmas Pageant

Chapter 9
ANNUAL EVENTS

January

Annual River Walk Mud Festival & Arts and Crafts Show
210-227-4262

This annual event coincides with the draining of the river for maintenance. An elected mud king and queen reign over the Mud Pie Ball and the Mud Parade. Arts and crafts line the River Walk. On weekdays, times are from 5-9 pm; weekends, 10 am-10 pm. Admission is free.

Cowboy Breakfast
210-479-3333

Take part in the world's largest free breakfast held at the Central Park Mall's parking lot. Held from 5 am-9 pm the 1st Saturday before the San Antonio Livestock Show and Rodeo. Over 55,000 attend this event that benefits lots of local scholarships.

February

San Antonio CineFestival
210-271-3151

Attend the oldest and largest Chicano and Latino film festival in the country—a huge filmmaker's conference. This five-day event takes place at the Guadalupe Cultural Arts Center's theater at different times of the year (February 28, 2001). Competitions include documentary, fiction, and experimental films. Admission to a screening is $6-8. Some screenings are free. One, in particular, caters to children. Call for more details.

San Antonio Stock Show and Rodeo
210-225-5851

The Stock Show and Rodeo begins each year with a Cowboy Breakfast that feeds 55,000 people fresh breakfast tacos and other tasty foods at the Central Park Mall. Twenty PRCA (Professional Rodeo Cowboy Association) rodeos, held at the Freemen Coliseum, feature big-name country, Tejano, and rock n' roll artists. Events include the Family Fair, shopping, and the livestock shows. Admission charged.

March

Dyeing O' the River Green Parade and Irish Show
210-497-8435

The San Antonio River becomes a River Shannon when 30 pounds of environmentally safe dye are dumped into it. A parade begins at La Mansion del Rio Hotel and proceeds to the Arneson Theater. More Irish entertainment takes place at the Arneson Theater. Free.

April

Fiesta San Antonio
210-227-5191

This 10-day citywide celebration is San Antonio's largest event, hosting 3.5 million visitors. The event includes carnivals, sports events, fireworks, musical entertainment, ethnic feasts, art exhibits, and parades—on the street and on the river. The festival, begun in 1891, honors Texas heroes and San Antonio's rich cultural heritage. It now features over 150 events such as Nights in Old San Antonio with 15 areas of food and entertainment that represent San Antonio's many ethnic influences (admission charged). The King William Fair features a parade, arts and crafts, musical entertainment, food, drinks, and more (free admission).

May

Annual Tejano Conjunto Festival en San Antonio
210-271-3151

Over 40,000 people attend the Guadalupe Cultural Arts Center's 6-day music festival, featuring 42 hours of live performances—with some of the best Tejano and conjunto musical groups in the country. Activities include a national poster contest, exhibits, and inductees into the Conjunto Music Hall of Fame. Enjoy accordion student recitals, food booths, games, and dancing. Events are held at Rose Dale Park at 340 Dartmouth Street and at the Guadalupe Theater. Admissions are good for an entire day, $6-8.

Cinco de Mayo Celebration
210-207-8600

Market Square celebrates the Battle of Pueblo, fought between the Mexican and the French forces that led to Mexico's independence. Sponsored by the Mexican American Cultural Center, the event is held on the closest weekend to the fifth of May with music, food, arts, and crafts. Free admission.

The Return of the Chili Queens
210-207-8600

Market Square relives the days of the famous Chili Queens as chili and other Mexican foods are served from tables set out on the open plazas, as it was in days past. Admission is free.

June

Concert Under the Stars
210-207-3255   www.sabot.org

Bring your lawn chairs or a blanket to sit on. Enjoy live musical entertainment while sitting in the lovely San Antonio Botanical Gardens. This series of concerts runs throughout the summer months. Call ahead and order lunch from Central Market. They will deliver for the event, 210-368-8600.

Shakespeare in the Park
210-226-2891

Arts! San Antonio features the best of Shakespeare, outdoors under the stars, at the San Antonio Botanical Gardens. Free: donations accepted.

Texas Folklife Festival
210-458-2300   www.texancultures.utsa.edu

Celebrate Texas' cultural and ethnic heritage with stories, crafts, music, dances, and goods. Educational and entertaining. Held at the Institute of Texas Cultures. Admission charged

---

July

Contemporary Art Month
210-227-6960

San Antonio focuses on its art community with over 70 events that involve more than 700 artists, performers, and musicians. Sponsored by the Blue Star Arts Complex.

September

Annual Jazz'SAlive
210-207-8486
A jazz festival with bands from New Orleans and San Antonio, held at Travis Park and sponsored by the San Antonio Parks Foundation and San Antonio Parks and Recreation Department. Enjoy arts, crafts, and food booths. Free admission.

Big Country River Festival
210-227-4262
Enjoy this music festival that includes an arts and crafts show. Held one weekend in late September at the River Walk's Arneson River Theater. Free admission.

Fiestas Patrias
210-207-8600
Market Square celebrates Diez y Seis, Mexico's independence from Spain, with entertainment and food. Sponsored by the Ladies LULAC Council 648. Free admission.

October

Inter-American Bookfair and Literary Festival
210-271-3151
The Guadalupe Cultural Arts Center's theater hosts the annual Inter-American Bookfair and Literary Festival. Focusing on Chicano, Latino, and Native

American writers, the festival features poetry and fiction readings, workshops, and book exhibits. Daytime events are free. Admission is charged for evening activities, $6-8. Opens on a Wednesday and runs through Saturday each October.

International Theatre Festival at San Antonio
210-227-0123
www.ci.si.sat.tx.us/daca

Theater companies from around the world celebrate for a weeklong festival of performances. Shows take place at the Majestic, Empire, and Cockrell Performance Theaters. And at the Beethoven Hall,

Oktoberfest San Antonio
210-222-1521

Enjoy authentic German food and drink at the Beethoven Haus and Gardens in the Historic King William District. Musical groups come from Munich, Germany, to entertain. Admission charged.

November

Feria de Santa Cecilia & Fiestas Navidenas
210-207-8600

See the lighting of Market Square that marks the beginning of the holiday season. Events include the Blessing of Animals and a visit from Pancho Claus. Free admission.

Lighting Ceremony
and River Walk Holiday Parade
210-227-4262

Held the Friday afterThanksgiving at 7 pm.Watch as over 100,000 lights switch on and light up the RiverWalk for the holidays.Activities include a parade of decorated boats that includes Santa's debut.Admission charge.

December

Fiesta de las Luminarias
210-227-4262

Candles, more than 2500 luminarias, line the walkways along the RiverWalk to symbolically light for the Holy Family. Sponsored by the Paseo del Rio Association. Free.

Las Posadas
210-224-6163

The Conservation Society presents an annual Spanish Christmas tradition of Joseph and Mary seeking a room at an inn—a religious drama from Mexico brought here by Franciscan friars in the 16th century. Children costumed as Joseph and Mary lead the candle-bearing procession that includes angels, shepherds, mariachis, and a choir.The procession begins at Crockett Street in front of the La Mansion del Rio Hotel.The public may join the procession or watch from the RiverWalk or near theArneson RiverTheater. Free admission.

Rivercenter Christmas Pageant
210-225-0000

River barges portray the Christmas story as they float into the Rivercenter Mall's lagoon and unfold a classic nativity scene. Admission is charged for reserved seating. Open seating is free.

Locations

1. Adam's Mark Hotel River Walk
2. Fairmount Hotel
3. Historic Camberley Gunter Hotel
4. Historic Menger Hotel
5. Historic Crown Plaza St. Anthony
6. Hilton Palacio del Rio
7. Holiday Inn Crocket Hotel
8. Holiday Inn River Walk
9. Homewood Suites River Walk
10. Hyatt Regency Hill Country Resort
11. La Mansion del Rio
12. Marriotts Riverwalk / Rivercenter
13. Plaza San Antonio
14. Riverwalk Inn Bed and Breakfast
15. Noble Inn
16. Oge House on the River Walk
17. Days Inn and Suites Fiesta Park
18. Fairfield Inn by Marriott
19. Hampton Inn Sea World
20. Holiday Inn Express
21. Radisson Market Square
22. Residence Inn Alamo Plaza
23. Super 8 Motel Six Flags Fiesta Texas
24. Admiralty Park
25. Dixie Kampground
26. Creek Hollow RV Park
27. Hill Country RV Park
28. Maricopa Ranch resort

Chapter 10
WHERE TO STAY?

Swanky, Upscale, and Famous Hotels in San Antonio

Bed and Breakfast Inns

Other Great Hotel and Motel Accommodations

R.V. Parks and Camping

SWANKY, UPSCALE, AND FAMOUS HOTELS

Adam's Mark Hotel RiverWalk

111 E. Pecan, 78205
800-444-2326 • 210-354-2800

The Adam's Mark Hotel offers 410 luxurious rooms and 4 suites. Amenities include in-room movies, two phone lines per room, an oversized working desk, a business center, an outdoor pool, a health club, a Jacuzzi, a gift shop, baby sitting, and laundry facilities. Their full service restaurant serves breakfast, lunch, and dinner.

Cost - $175-900

Directions - From I-35 exit Main Street and go south. Turn left on Pecan Street. The hotel will be on Soledad, between E. Martin and Pecan Streets.

Fairmount Hotel

401 S. Alamo, 78205
210-224-8800

The Fairmount Hotel sets a record in the Guinness Book of World Records. Its trek across town is recorded as "the heaviest building ever moved on wheels." At the same time, an excavation of its present location revealed many artifacts used during the Battle of the Alamo. The hotel now sits on a State Archaeological Landmark and displays the findings.

Built in 1906, it originated as a hotel for railway travelers. Now meticulously restored, this small red brick and limestone luxury hotel, with Italianate Victorian architecture, specializes in personal service. Enjoy staying in one of their plush 19 guestrooms or 17 suites. The hotel considers itself a "country-style bed and breakfast within the city limits."

Cost - $183-550

Directions - Across from the HemisFair Plaza.

Historic Camberley Gunter Hotel

205 E. Houston 78205
210-227-3241

Treat yourself any morning at Gunter Hotel's bakery and enjoy some of the finest baked goods in San Antonio. This classy hotel sits across the street from the Majestic Theatre and features lots of family amenities: a swimming pool, an exercise room, a gift shop, a barbershop, a child-sitting service, a full-service dining room, and a shoe shine. Note the Swiss-German décor and the art that hangs in the hotel, particularly the one over the staircase on the third floor—they're originals. For valet parking use the entrance on St. Mary's and Travis Streets. Conveniently located in downtown San Antonio.

Cost - $119-350

Directions - Corner of E. Houston and St. Mary's.

Historic Menger Hotel

204 Alamo 78205
800-345-9285   210-223-4361

Built in 1859 as the finest hotel west of the Mississippi, the Menger's history includes many famous people: Ulysses S. Grant, Robert E. Lee, Sarah Bernhardt, and Oscar Wilde. Still as charming today, the hotel offers a self-guided tour. See the ballroom, note the artwork, walk the hallways. Ask the front desk for a pamphlet. Modern amenities at the Menger Hotel: an outdoor heated pool, a hot tub, a spa, an exercise room, a valet laundry, restaurant, a shopping arcade, and a gift shop.

Cost - $112-550

Directions - Between the Alamo and Rivercenter Mall.

Historic Crown Plaza St. Anthony

300 E. Travis 78205
800-277-6963 • 210-227-4392

Stay in a hotel designated a Texas and National Landmark. Built in 1909, the St. Anthony is known for elegance and old-world style. See many French Empire antiques and original oils and watercolors by such artists as Remington, Cartier, and DeYoung. The lobby features an eight-foot French chandelier, hand-painted Mexican tiles, and priceless Chinese vases.

The St. Anthony is located across the street from historic Travis Park and one block from the River Walk. Walk to many of the attractions in downtown from the hotel. I truly enjoyed staying here.

Cost - $140-275

Directions - From I-37 exit Commerce Street and go left. Turn right on Navarro Street, then right on Travis Street. The hotel will be on the corner of Navarro and Travis Streets.

Hilton Palacio del Rio

200 S. Alamo 78205
800 Hiltons 210-222-1400

This 22-story hotel set a record, opening in only

202 days for the 1968 World's Fair. With aggressive planning, the hotel used precast concrete modules—500 furnished bedrooms, weighing 35 tons—all ready to hoist in to place. You'll enjoy staying at this 4-Diamond hotel located right on the River Walk. Best of all, children under 18 stay free with their parents or even grandparents. All rooms offer private balconies with a fantastic view. Other hotel features include an outdoor swimming pool (on the roof), a hot tub, a fitness room, a full-service business center, valet parking, and laundry facilities. Transportation to the airport leaves every 40 minutes for $6.

Cost - $201-775

Directions - Across from the entrance to HemisFair Park.

Holiday Inn Crockett Hotel
320 Bonham 78205
210-225-6500

History and location make the Crockett Hotel a novelty. Situated next to the Alamo, this 100-year-old 7-story hotel is located in in the historic part of downtown San Antonio. Guests easily walk to many of the attractions like the River Walk or the Rivercenter Mall. The décor includes a southwestern flavor with pine furnishings and artwork depicting regional history. The upper stories' view of downtown can't be beat. Enjoy the rooftop hot tub and the swimming pool. Compared to others downtown, the hotel is smaller and unpretentious, with 206 rooms.

Cost - $109-159

Directions - Next to the Alamo.

Holiday Inn River Walk

217 N. St. Mary's St. 78205
800-465-4329 • 210-224-2500

Kids under 12 eat free anytime at the Holiday Inn River Walk's restaurant, Fandangos. The hotel is located on the River Walk and conveniente to most of the downtown attractions. Family amenities include a game room, a swimming pool, an exercise room, a whirlpool, and a gift shop. Rooms feature king beds and extra work space. Suites offer refrigerators.

Cost - $125-275

Directions - From I-37 South, exit Commerce/ Alamo. Turn right on Commerce, then right on Soledad, then left on Houston to N. St. Mary's.

Homewood Suites River Walk

432 West Market 78205
800-225-5466 • 210-222-1515

Homewood Suites—one of the best bets for any family wanting to visit San Antonio. Enjoy a view of the river with your complimentary continental breakfast that includes cereal, waffles, pancakes, bagels, fruit, juices, and more. Evenings include a 2-hour social featuring a complimentary light meal or snacks.

Suites come with 1 or 2 bedrooms, a living room, and a fully equipped kitchen with a microwave, a full refrigerator, a dishwasher, dining tables, plates, silverware, pots, and pans. Located within walking distance of most attractions.

Cost - $99-169 Suites

Directions - Located on Market and St. Mary's.

Hyatt Regency Hill Country Resort

9800 Hyatt Regency Dr. 78251
800-233-1234 • 210-647-1234

The Hyatt Regency Hill Country Resort is a 200-acre family retreat. Kids tube in their 950-foot Ramblin' River and splash in a shallow pool April through October, weather permitting. Camp Hyatt's crafts, hiking, and swimming, for kids while parents enjoy the adult amenities. Call and make reservations at least 72 hours in advance. The resort offers tennis, golf, an exercise room, a fitness center, a swimming pool, and 3 full restaurants.

Suites come with one or two bedrooms. It is located minutes away from SeaWorld.

Cost - $255-660

Directions - Take I-10 West to 90 West to 151 West. Go approximately 15 minutes to the resort..

La Mansion del Rio Hotel

112 College St. 78205
800-292-7300 • 210-225-2581

Stay where celebrities like to stay in San Antonio. Built in 1854 as a catholic boys' school it converted to a hotel in time for the World's Fair. Unique in its design, the hotel features an old-world Spanish courtyard. Considered a historic treasure, it is located on the River Walk and within walking distance of the Convention Center and the Alamo. Amenities include valet parking, an attached parking garage, a ballroom, a gift shop, plush rooms, and great service.

Cost - $210-1900

Directions - Located at the corner of College Street and Navarro or St. Mary's Streets.

Marriotts Riverwalk/Rivercenter

101 Bowie St. 78295
800-228-9290 • 210-223-1000

Every tree along the River Walk lights up for the holidays. Get a spectacular view from your own balcony facing the river at the **Marriott Riverwalk Hotel.** Or simply watch the sun set. You'll find the best view in town from their rooms. Balconies come with chairs, tables, and room service.

Because the **Marriott Rivercenter** is connected with the Rivercenter Mall, enjoy shopping over at 100 stores. Other family amenities include babysitting, a fast-food court, indoor-outdoor swimming pools, a whirlpool, an executive health club, saunas, parking, a gift shop, and restaurants.

Cost - $209-$450

Directions - (These Marriotts are located next to each other.) From 281, exit Commerce Street and go west 1 block. The hotels will be on the right.

Plaza San Antonio

555 S. Alamo St. 78205
210-229-1000

Imagine relaxing at a spacious resort hotel in busy downtown San Antonio. The Plaza San Antonio, the only downtown hotel with tennis courts, sits on 6 lush acres. See the free-roaming exotic birds: peacocks and Chinese pheasants. Enjoy the health club, the swimming pool, valet parking, and in-room service. Best of all, the hotel is located two blocks from the River Walk and three from the Alamo. Considered a world-class hotel, the Plaza San Antonio rates as "one of the top 25 in the country"— 4 Diamond, 4 Stars—with award-winning catering.

Cost - $199-$370

Directions - On S. Alamo and E. Durango Streets, across the street from the HemisFair Park.

BED AND BREAKFAST INNS

Riverwalk Inn Bed and Breakfast

329 Old Guilbeau, 78204 800-254-4440

www.riverwalkinn.com

What happens when you reassemble log cabins from Tennessee along the River Walk? You get a lot of charm at this bed and breakfast inn. Five 19th-century log homes came to San Antonio from Tennessee—log by log. Enjoy sitting on the porch in a rocker or in front of the fireplace when it's cold out. Beds come with old-fashioned quilts and rooms with country antiques. Your stay includes a continental breakfast sitting at a rustic antique table. Every afternoon, a freshly baked snack awaits you as you come in from sightseeing. Believe me, when your vacation is over, you won't want to leave.

Cost

Rooms with river view

Weekdays . . . . $110-$130
Weekends . . . . $130-$160

Directions

From 281, exit Durango St./Alamo dome. Stay in the right-hand lane and turn right on Durango. Go .8 mile, crossing S. Alamo and S. St. Mary's Streets and turn right on Aubrey St. The inn will be on the corner of Aubrey and Guilbeau Streets.

Noble Inns

Jackson House
107 Madison 78204

Pancoast Carriage House
202 Washington Street 78204
210-225-4045
www.nobleinns.com

Let the Noble Inns know and they will pick you up at the airport in their classic 1960 Rolls Royce Silver Cloud II. Stay in the heart of the King William District in 100-year-old Victorian homes meticulously restored and designated as historical landmarks. Choose between the Pancoast Carriage House and the Jackson House. Each offers fresh flowers, guest robes, linen, daily maid service, and more. Rooms come with Victorian antiques, fireplaces, private marble baths, and modern amenities such as phones, cable TV, air-conditioning, and dataports. The inns are conveniently located within walking distance of many downtown attractions.

Cost

Weekdays	$115-$175
Weekends	$130-$190

Directions

For the Jackson House, from Durango Street turn right on S. St. Mary's and turn right again on Madison Street. For the Pancoast Carriage, take Durango Street past S. St. Mary's and go left on Pancoast. The street forks, take Washington Avenue. The inn will be the first driveway on the left.

Oge House Inn on the River Walk

209 Washington Street, 78204

210-223-2353

www.ogeinn.com

The Oge House, a 19th-century mansion, is listed as a Texas Historical Landmark and on the National Register of Historic Places. Built in 1837 and once owned by Texas Ranger Louis Oge, the house now serves as a charming bed and breakfast inn in the King William Historical District. Each room and suite offers a private bath; most have fireplaces. Enjoy modern conveniences: telephones, cable TV, refrigerators. Eat breakfast either in the formal dining room or on the veranda. Catch the streetcar a few blocks away for all the attractions.

Cost

$145-205

Directions

From I-37, take the Durango/Alamodome exit and go left on Durango. Go through 4 stop lights and turn left after St. Mary's onto Pancoast Street. The Inn will be the 1st house on your right. Park behind the hedge.

OTHER GREAT HOTEL AND MOTEL ACCOMMODATIONS

Days Inn and Suites Fiesta Park
11790 I-10 West 78230
800-329-7466 210-696-7922

Fairfield Inn by Marriott
620 S. Santa Rosa 78204
800-228-2800 210-299-1000

Hampton Inn Sea World
4803 Manitou 78228
210-684-9966

Holiday Inn Express Hotel & Suites
524 S. St. Mary's 78205
800-969-3239 210-354-1333

Radisson Market Square
502 W. Durango 78207
210-224-7155

Residence Inn Alamo Plaza
425 Bonham 78205
800-331-3131 210-212-5555

Super 8 Motel Six Flags Fiesta Texas
5319 Casa Bella (I-10 West) 78249
800-800-8000 210-696-6916

RV PARKS AND CAMPING

Admiralty Park

1485 N. Ellison Dr., San Antonio, 78251 • 210-647-7878

Offers a free shuttle to SeaWorld, near Fiesta Texas. offers 240 concrete pads, a pool, a Jacuzzi, cable TV, free movies.

Dixie Kampground

1011 Gembler Rd., San Antonio 78219 • 210-337-6501

Cabins and camping spaces. Old pecan trees, pool, Jacuzzi, and store. Minutes from downtown. Between I-35N and I-10W. From I-10 exit W.W. White going north. Then left on Gembler.

Creek Hollow RV Park

40970 FM 3159, Canyon Lake 78133
830-899-7121

In the scenic Hill Country with an abundant of wildlife and trees. Golf, boating, rafting, and fishing nearby. Take 281 to 46 going east to 3159 northeast.

Hill Country RV Park

131 Ruekle Road, New Braunfels 78130
830-625-1919

Five minutes from downtown New Braunfels or 30 miles north of San Antonio. Amenities include 300 full hookups and pull: throughs, cable, phones, heated pool, sauna, hot tub, exercise room, and recreation room.

Maricopa Ranch Resort

12915 Hwy 306, Canyon Lake 78130 • 830-964-3731

Convenient to lake and river for tubing, canoeing, fishing, and swimming. Has 140 full hookup sites, cottages with kitchenettes, swimming pool and spa. Take I-35 north and exit 191. Go left 14 miles. Will be on the left.

Locations

1. Brackenridge Park
2. Cedar Creek
3. Misson del Lago
4. Olmos Basin Golf Course
5. Riverside Golf Course
6. Willow Springs Golf Course
7. La Cantera Golf Course
8. SilverHorn Golf Course
9. The Quarry Golf Course
10. Hyatt Regency Country Resort
11. Tapatio Springs Resort & Conference Center

Chapter 11
GOLF COURSES
IN THE SAN ANTONIO AREA

MUNICIPAL COURSES

Brackenridge Park
2315 Avenue B, San Antonio 78218
210-226-5612

Golf at the oldest public course in the state. Designed by the legendary A.W. Tillinghast, this 18-hole hosted the 1st Texas Open in 1922. Having 6185 yards (men) and 5216 (women) the course's front nine is lined with oaks and pecans. Players' tee shots must be accurate to score well. The back nine is open but often windy. Slope 122 Rating 67 Par 72. Weekdays $14, weekends $17, cart $18.

Cedar Creek
8050 Vista Colina, San Antonio 78255
210-695-5050

A top-ranking municipal 18-hole course in South Texas. Scenic Cedar Creek's course winds through limestone hillsides taking golfers up and down steep elevations, around several waterfalls and creeks. Different levels of greens make it challenging. With 7158 (men) and 5535 (women), Slope 132, Rating 73.4, Par 72. Weekdays and weekends $44, includes carts.

Mission del Lago
1250 Mission Grande, San Antonio 78214
210-627-2522

This 18-hole course is flat, but the Texas wind makes it more challenging. Other difficulties—water on 10 of the holes and subtle greens—test any player's ability, particularly on the back tees. With 7004 yards (men) and 5748 (women), Slope 127. Rating 72.6, Par 72. Weekdays $32, weekends $39. Prices include carts.

Olmos Basin Golf Course
7022 N. McCullough, San Antonio 78216
210-826-4041

As one of San Antonio's most popular 18-hole courses, the Olmos Basin Golf Course offers several demanding par 3 holes. The course is fairly straightforward in design—nothing too tricky for a good golfer. With 6896 yards (men) and 5748 (women), Slope 123, Rating 71.0 Par 72. Weekdays $16, weekends $19, carts $18.

Riverside Golf Course
203 McDonald, San Antonio 78210
210-533-8371

Teddy Roosevelt and his Rough Riders trained at this site. This 18-hole course offers an all par 3 course, plus a full-size 18-hole championship course (6694 yards men, 5730, women). With trees lining the fairways, it's a straight hitter's advantage. The back nine is for the long hitters. Slope 128, Rating 72, Par 72. Weekdays $16, weekends $19, and carts $18.

Willow Springs Golf Course
202 Coliseum Road, San Antonio 78219
210-226-6721

Willow Springs features the longest hole in San Antonio- a 663-yard par-5 second hole. Hosting many Texas Opens with famous players like Ben Hogan and Bryon Nelson, this 18-hole course is noted for challenging par 4s. With 7221 (men) and 5792 (women), Slope 134, Rating 73.9, Par 72. Weekdays $14, weekends $17, and carts $16.

PUBLIC AND DAILY FEE COURSES

La Cantera Golf Club

16641 La Cantera Parkway, San Antonio 78256
210 558-4653 • 800-446-5387

Designed by Jay Morrish and Tom Weiskopf, La Cantera rates as the "best public course" in Texas, hosting the Texas Open four years in a row. Golfers tee up and down on a scenic multi-tiered range. An 18-hole course with 7001 yards (men) and 4940 (women), Slope 132 Rating 72.5, Par 72. Weekdays $110, Weekends $125.

SilverHorn Golf Club

1100 W. Bitters Road, San Antonio 78216
210-545-5300

San Antonio's newest course designed by a well-known architect Randy Heckenkemper, with help from PGA tour pros Scott Verplank and Willie Wood. Perhaps San Antonio's finest course, heavily forested with rolling hills, the SilverHorn Golf Club has a 7000-yard layout with 262 acres. Yards: Gold 6922; Black 5831; Silver 5271. Rating Championship 73.1, Gold 70.6, Black 68.4 Silver 66.4. Fees: $75 includes cart during the week and $79.95 on weekends.

Quarry Golf Club
444 East Basse Road, San Antonio, 78209
210-824-4500

Its back nine sits in an old limestone quarry framed by 100-foot bluffs. Named in Golfweek Magazine as "America's Best—#2" and in Golf Digest as "Best Course—#4 in Texas." Many par 4s are tough. The windy front nine—designed like the British Open links-style courses—challenge any golfer. With 6740 yards (men) and 4897 (women), Slope 128, Rating 72.4, Par 71. Weekdays $95, weekends $110. Price includes the cart.

RESORTS

Hyatt Regency Hill Country Resort
9800 Hyatt Resort Dr.
San Antonio, 78251 210-520-4040

Designed by Arthur Hill, this 18-hole course will challenge any player. Scenic with trees and a Hill Country atmosphere. Yards: 6913 (men), 4781 (women). Slope 136, Rating 73.9, Par 72. Fee: $120—includes cart. After 3pm, the twilight fee is $70.

Tapatio Springs Resort & Conference Center
I-10 West to Exit #539
Johns Road, Boerne, TX
210-696-3539 800-999-3299

Three spectacular 9-hole Hill Country golf courses with splendid views. Play any combination. Will challenge any player, with water on 14 of the holes. Yardage, slope, par vary according to the combination of 9-holes played. Weekdays $83, weekends $95, includes cart.

Chapter 12
NEW BRAUNFELS AND THE GUADALUPE RIVER

ANTIQUE SHOPS

New Braunfels—known as the "Antique Capital of Texas". Considered world-class shopping for antique lovers. You'll find antique shops well priced. Many locate on San Antonio Street within walking distance of each other. The following are favorites:

Downtowner Antique Mall

223 San Antonio St., New Braunfels
830 629-3947

An antique mall with 15 dealers each with their own specialties. A fun place to browse. Opens at 10 am. Closed on Tuesdays.

Gruene Antique Co.

1607 Hunter Road, New Braunfels
830-629-7781

One of the largest and most well-known places to shop for antiques in the area. The 8000-square-foot store features 30 different collectors and dealers. Offers furniture to small serving items. Located in the Gruene Historic District; housed in the H. B. Gruene's Mercantile Building — a Texas landmark. Opens at 10 am

Headrick Antiques

697 S. Seguin, New Braunfels 78130
830-625-1624

Specializing in "real" antiques. Their motto is: "Where browsing is fun and acquiring is exciting. " You'll find Early American and Texas Colonial handmade furniture. Opens at 10 am.

CHILDREN'S MUSEUM

651 Business Loop I-35, Suite 530
New Braunfels 78130
830-620-0939

Children's Museum features New Braunfels' culture

Learn as you play. Reign in a castle (like the one in New Braunfels, Germany). Explore Grandma's attic (Oma's Dachboden), and turn butter or wash with a washboard. Pretend you're a doctor, dress up as a princess or a fireman or a cowboy. Listen to stories and peep through a microscope. The hands-on displays at the Children's Museum will brighten any child's day.

Annual family memberships offer unlimited admission for very little, $35.

Hours

Mon. – Sat.	9 am – 5 pm
Thursday	until 8 pm
Sunday	Noon – 5 pm

Cost

Per person	$3
Members	Free

Directions

From I-35, take exit #189.
Will be in the New Braunfels Marketplace.

CHRISTMAS CAROLING IN THE CAVERNS

26495 Natural Bridge Caverns Road
Natural Bridge Caverns 78266
210-651-6101

Make this an annual holiday activity

Delight your whole family with this holiday fun thing to do. For three weekends in December, the Natural Bridge Caverns open for a caroling tour.

Enjoy hearing your favorite Christmas carol resounding through the cavern of this underground cave. It's spectacular. The pathway to the caverns sparkle with Christmas lights.

Local restaurants cater meals for this event. Guests are led through the caverns as local church and school choirs in various caverns are singing. The cavern's acoustics make this a memorable evening.

You can choose to take the combined dinner and tour or the tour only.

The proceeds from this event help support many of the local charities in New Braunfels.

Hours

Three weekends in December,
Call for more information and reservations

Cost includes dinner

Adults $30
Children ages 4-12 .... $19
Seniors $27

Directions

From San Antonio, take I-35N. to exit #175 (Natural Bridge Caverns Road) FM 3009 and go east 8 miles.

GRISTMILL RIVER RESTAURANT

1287 Gruene Road
Gruene 78130
830-625-0684

A fun place to eat

    Dine outdoors in the ruins of an old 1800's cotton gin overlooking the Guadalupe River. Specialties include extra large fries cut in round slices, South Texas polish sausage cooked in barbecue sauce, grilled fillet with cracked black peppers, and marinated grilled chicken breast. Or try their Gristburger with spicy queso sauce. Top this off with their pecan pie or the Hill Country Strawberry Shortcake.

    In Gruene, the Gristmill River Restaurant sits directly behind the 100-year old dance hall and under the town's water tower. The restaurant features a retail store with Gristmill hats, mugs, and t-shirts.

Hours

Summer

Daily . . . . 11 am - 11 pm

Winter

Sun - Thurs. . . . . 11 am - 9 pm
Fri - Sat . . . . 11 am - 10 pm

Cost

$4.50 - $13.99

Directions

From I-35, exit 191 and go west 1.5 miles and then turn left on Hunter Road. Travel .5 miles to Gruene.

GRUENE HISTORIC DISTRICT
Hunters Road, Gruene 78130
830-629-5077

In the 1840's, German farmers settled along the banks of the Guadalupe River, 4 miles out of New Braunfels in Gruene. The first mercantile store opened in 1878, close to the cotton gin along the Guadalupe River. After that came the dance hall and many others during this prosperous time. In the 1920's, the depression and the boll weevil turned the community into a ghost town. Today, the unique buildings of Gruene are listed on the National Register of Historic Places. The town is a thriving tourist attraction.

Places you'll want to see: **Gruene General Store**, an authentic general store with soda fountain, and **BushWhackers**, selling fine furniture made from discarded wood pieces. Others favorites include the **Lone Star Country Store**, **Buck Pottery, Cotton-Eyed Joe's**, the **Gristmill River Restaurant**, and the **Gruene Mansion Restaurant**. Down on the banks of the river, rent tubes and rafts for a float on the Guadalupe River at the **Rockin R River Rides**, one of the largest river outfits in the area. Rentals include shuttle rides. 830-629-999

The oldest dance hall in Texas, the **Gruene Hall,** features the best in country, blues, and folk musicians. Many like George Strait, Lyle Lovett, and the Fabulous Thunderbirds have played here.

Hours
(Store hours vary with extended hours in the summer)
Daily . . . . 9 am – 6 pm

Directions
From I-35, take exit 191 (FM 306) west 1.5 miles to Hunter's Road and go left.

GUADALUPE RIVER SCENIC AREA
canoeing, rafting, tubing

River Road
New Braunfels, Texas
830-964-3342 ex. I (GuadalupeRiver information)

The Guadalupe River's a haven for tubers. Drive this scenic River Road, a 15-mile stretch from the city limits of New Braunfels (Loop 337) to Sattler, just below the Canyon Lake Dam. The road meanders along side the Guadalupe River, crossing it four times. Here you'll find one of the most popular spots in Texas for recreation; in fact, 35,000 people tube the river during the Labor Day weekend.

Banks of the river are dotted with outfits that rent tubes, rafts, and canoes, and designated put-ins and take-outs. Tubes rent for $9-10 and include a shuttle ride back. Some tubes come with plastic bottoms for toting smaller kids and ice chests. The Canyon Dam controls water levels; but drought years favor smaller children and flood levels challenge the kayakers. Waters in between please everyone else.

Here is a favorite outfitter and place to stay along the river.

River Valley Resort & Rio Raft Co.

PO Box 2036, Canyon Lake 78130
830-964-3613
www.riviervalleyresort.net

Stay with the nicest folks on the river

Located on a scenic bank of the Guadalupe River with bluffs and huge oaks, pecans, cypress, and junipers, the River Valley Resort offers all the amenities you'll need for a super outing. Rent a tidy cottage: the smallest sleeps 4, the largest 8; park your RV or put up a tent along the water's front. Rent a tube or take a raft trip that includes a shuttle ride and life vests.

The convenience store supplies guests with ice, cold drinks, sunscreen, souvenirs, and snacks. This family-oriented resort prides itself on personal service. Popular in the winter with Winter Texans and fly fishermen and in the summer with family reunions. Call ahead 2 or 3 months for reservations.

On the first weekend in October the resort features an authentic Native American Pow Wow. You'll want to attend. Many tribes from around the country—a gathering of nations—celebrate their cultural heritage. Enjoy Indian dancing, arts, crafts, and food booths.

Office hours

Daily .... 9 am – 4 pm

Cost

Tube rental .... $9-$10
Standard Raft Trips
Adults $19
Children under 12 .... $16
Short Raft Trips
Adults $15
Children under 12 .... $12

(Winter rates are lower)

Cabins $75-180
RV Sites $20-23
Camping $18

Directions

From I-35, exit # 191 (FM 306) and travel 13 miles west. Turn left on FM 2673 and go 1½ miles to River Road. Turn left and go 1 mile. Will be on the left.

LANDA PARK

City of New Braunfels Parks and Recreation
110 Golf Course Drive
New Braunfels 78130
830-608-2160

New Braunfels' best-kept secret

This 300-acre park complex, including Prince Solms Park, bursts with things to do. The crystal-clear Comal River, perhaps the shortest river in the world, begins in Landa Park, and flows 2½ miles before emptying into the Guadalupe. Grab your tube for a float or a slide down the Prince Solms Tube Chute. Haven't got a tube? Rent one from the park.

Many of the activities available include an arboretum with 96 species of trees—some over 300 years old, an 18-hole golf course, shaded picnic facilities along the Comal River, an Olympic-size swimming pool, a spring-fed pool, a miniature train, and a miniature golf course. The park rents paddle boats and glass-bottom boats, too. Here's a great place for walking or jogging. Feed the ducks. Go fishing.

Summers include Thursday night concerts in the park.

Hours

Hours for the different attractions vary
Daily .... 6 am - midnight

Cost

Varies for the attraction

Directions

From I-35 take exit #187 (Seguin Street) and go north through the city's plaza. Continue on Seguin until you reach Landa Drive and go left. Watch for entrance to the park.

MUSEUM OF TEXAS HANDMADE FURNITURE

1370 Churchhill Dr., New Braunfels 78130
830-629-6504

Fine furniture built by German pioneer craftsmen

This unique museum centers on the area's fine pioneer furniture. From as early as 1845, many German immigrant cabinetmakers settled in the Hill Country. Names of these early woodworking settlers include Scholl, Tietze, Jahn, Stautzenberger, Holtz, and Ebensberger. See original furniture handmade in Texas from the 1860's to the mid-19th century. Housed in the Breustedt Haus, a Texas historic landmark, the museum contains rare and interesting items used in the area's pioneer homes.

The museum includes a log cabin and a one-room cabin furnished with tools and furniture of the early pioneers. Tours are given as visitors come and last an hour. The last tour begins at 3:30 pm.

Hours

Closed Mondays, January, and February

Tues. – Sun. 1 pm–4 pm

Costs

Adults $5
Children (6-12) $1
Children (under 6) . . . . Free

Directions

Take I-35N. and exit #189 (Highway 46, Loop 337). Go west through two lights. Turn right on Churchill Dr. The museum is on the right.

NAEGELIN'S BAKERY

129 S. Seguin Street
New Braunfels, 78130 830-625-5722

Fine German pastries from Texas' oldest bakery

You must try the apple struedel. It's authentic like that found in the old country—and the tastiest in Texas. And of couse, you enjoy the lebkuchen and other fine German treats too.

This is the oldest bakery in Texas. It dates back to 1868 and originally located on Mill and Seguin Streets in the old Goldenbegen House. The Naegelin Family bought the bakery from a baker who once baked for a German prince named Heinrich Zuschlag. In 1870, the bakery was moved to its present location on South Seguin.

Many of the old tools once used to make the breads, cookies, and pastries are on display at the local Sophienburg Museum. See the old dough cutter, the rolling pin, the large sifter, cook cutters, and more.

The Naegelin Family operated this bakery for three generations and then sold it to the Granzin Family. The recipes used today are the original baker's.

Hours

Mon.–Fri. . . . . 6:30 am – 5:30 pm
Saturday . . . . 6:30 am – 5 pm

Cost

One slice apple struedel $1.10

Direction

Located downtown New Braunfels on the Plaza.

NEW BRAUNFELS GOLF COURSES

Golf at one of these courses open to the public. Fees vary according to season. Call for times.

Canyon Lake Golf Course & Country Club

FM 2673 to Startzville, Canyon Lake
830-899-3301

Located 30 minutes from San Antonio. A scenic course with lots of trees and hills that's challenging for the yardage. Semi-private.

Yards: 6016 men, 4726 women.

Slope 122, Rating 68.8, Par 72.

Fees: weekdays $21, weekends $30 including cart.

Landa Park Municipal Golf Course

800 Golf Course Drive, New Braunfels 78130
830-608-2174

One of the busiest courses in Texas. The Landa Park Municipal Golf Course features a traditional wide open, user friendly 18-hole course. The Comal River runs through it.

Yards: 6103 men, 4919 women.

Slope 112, Rating 68.9, Par 72.

Fees: weekdays $12.50, weekends $15.75, cart $19.

Long Creek Home of the Bandit

6019 FM 725, New Braunfels 78130
830-609-4665

A championship golf course in a beautiful hill country setting. Wide open with 100 foot elevation. Water on 11 of the 18 holes. Challenging. Four sets of tees.

Yards: 6928 men, 5253 women.

Slope 133, Rating 73.6. Par 71.

Fees: weekdays $50, weekends $62, including cart.

NEW BRAUNFELS MUSEUM OF ART

199 Main Plaza
New Braunfels 78130
830-625-5636 or 800-456-4866

See their huge Hummel figuine collection and Texas folk art

Many of the Hummel figurines in this collection are worth thousands of dollars.

As a nun in Germany during World War II, Sister Hummel created her many priceless art pieces, capturing the innocence of humanity. See the largest collection of her original artwork that inspired the Hummel figurines: her charcoals, pastels, oils. Don't miss the 45-minute video about her.

Diversified, this museum is also dedicated to famous living Texas artists and musicians. This museum lets you experience the most talented Texas artists. If you love folk art, stop here.

Hours

Mon. – Sat. . . . . 10 am-5 pm

Cost

Adults $5
Students (18-6) $3
Children (under 6) . . . . Free
Seniors $4.50

Directions

Take exit #187 from I-35N and follow Seguin Ave. to the town circle; veer to the right 1/4 around the circle. The museum in next to the courthouse.

SCHLITTERBAHN WATERPARK AND RESORTS

400 N. Liberty
New Braunfels
830-625-2351
www.schlitterbahn.com

Huge Texas-size water park

See what hi-tech did to a Texas water park. You must ride the Master Blaster, the Schlitterbahn's award-winning, one-of-a-kind uphill water coaster. Fun. Fun. Fun. Of course it's popular—plan to get in line first thing in the morning.

One of my most favorite places to go, the Schlitterbahn with its German culture and heritage features a 65-acre water park and a resort complex. You'll find over 40 rides and 6 theme areas. Enjoy 3 uphill water coasters—a must-do, 9 tube chutes, 17 water slides, 5 children's water play areas and a tidal wave river. The resort ranges in accommodations from motel rooms, condos, and cottages to furnished homes. Plan ahead to stay here.

This fantastic water park, the largest and most popular in the world, hosts over 800,000 people during their summer season. Peak times for crowds run from July 1 – August 10. Lines get long,but, the park is extremely well run.

Don't forget to bring a cooler with food for lunch, a tradition at the Schlitterbahn. Grab yourself a table, there are hundreds throughout the park. This is the only large attraction in Texas that allows food and drinks into the park. Or eat lunch at the concessions and restaurants available.

Parking, inner tubes, life vests, and bodyboards are free. Group discounts available as well as season passes. Don't forget the sunscreen.

Hours

Open weekends late April through mid-May and late August through mid-September.

Open Daily mid-May through mid-August.

Call or check website for schedule.

Cost

(Season passe available)

Call or check website for rates.

Directions

From San Antonio, take IH-35 North to New Braunfels. On the north side of New Braunfels take exit 189 and go west on loop 337/Hwy 46. Go left on Common Street.

To main park Castle entrance: Stay on Common to liberty Street. Go right on Liberty to main entrance on left side of street, Parkin attendants will direct you to the nearest parking lots.

SOPHEINBURG MUSEUM AND ARCHIVES

401 West Coll Street
New Braunfels 78130
830-629-1572

A history teaching museum

One large trunk weighing no more than 500lbs. came with each German family to settle New Braunfels. Items brought often included the men's work tools that greatly influenced the area. Many families donated these pioneer artifacts to this museum devoted to local family histories. Very interesting, a must-see. The archives at 200 N. Seguin brag of having over a million old photos, old newspapers, oral history accounts, and maps. Their hours are Mon. - Fri., 10 am - 4 pm.

Wander through the museum; plan to spend at least an hour. With ten or more in your group, schedule a tour. Smaller groups may join others.

Hours

Mon. – Sat. .... 10 am – 5 pm
Sunday .... 1 pm – 5 pm

Cost

Adults $5
Students 18 and under .... Free
Members .... Free

Directions

From San Antonio, take I-35 North and exit Sequin Street. Go left under the freeway towards downtown New Braunfels. Turn left on Coll Street. Go up the hill, will be on the right.

THE NEW BRAUNFELS SMOKEHOUSE

146 Highway 46 E.
New Braunfels 78130
830-625-2416

The New Braunfels Smokehouse, an eating tradition since 1945

A visit to New Braunfels wouldn't be complete without a stop at the New Braunfels Smokehouse. Serving fine home-style breakfasts, lunches, and dinners. During the summer months, enjoy breakfast and barbecue buffets in the Yard. Try their Chicken and Dumplings, one of their specialties, or the Smoked Baby Back Ribs. Don't forget the bread pudding. Before you leave, stock up at their deli with high quality cheeses smoked meats: bacon, jerky, hams, sausages, rib. Better yet, pick up a catalog; they ship anywhere in the U.S.

The delightful decor consists of early Texas antiques. Their gift shop sells gourmet foods, cookbooks, kitchen gifts, handmade items, and more.

Hours

(Closes at 8 pm during winter months)
Daily . . . . 7:30 am – 9 pm

Cost

$6.29 - 12.95

Directions

At the corner of Highway 46 and I-35N. Exit 189.

THE RESTAURANT AT GRUENE MANSION

1275 Gruene Road
New Braunfels 78131
830-620-0760

Newly opened, the Gruene Mansion Restaurant offers fine dining in a beautiful settling. Eat out on the breezy decks facing the Guadalupe River or inside the mansion with the huge rock fireplace. Order one of their fantastic salads. Other exceptional entrees include their Chicken Oporto, the Grilled Salmon, and the New Braunfels Smoked Sausage. They serve tasty pasta dishes and gourmet sandwiches, too. Kids under 10 will enjoy their child's menu. Popular for weddings and catered events. Enjoy live music on Friday and Saturday evenings.

Come during the holidays, when the restaurant is spectacularly decorated in red and gold—it takes them three weeks to put it together.

Hours

Mon.–Fri. . . . . 5pm– 10 pm
Saturday . . . . 11 am–10 pm
Sunday . . . . 10 am–10 pm

Cost

Entrees . . . . $8.95 - 19.95

Directions

From I-35, exit 191 (FM 306) west 1.5 miles to Hunter's Road and go left.

WURSTFEST

178 Landa Park Drive, New Braunfels 78130
830-625-9167 • 800-221-4369

New Braunfels' famous festival

New Braunfels' Wurstfest—a ten-day salute to sausage—rates as "one of the top events in North America." Over 100,000 people attend this festival that begins on the first Friday before the first Monday in November.

Enjoy the best of German food and entertainment: oompah bands, singers, dancers, yodelers, and polkas. Each year, the Wurstfest features a brass band from Germany. Other bands and entertainers like Myron Floren from the Lawrence Welk Show come from around the country to perform each year. With over 40 food booths, eats at the festival includes imported wursts, sausages on a stick, turkey legs, sauerkrauts, potato pancakes, and more.

The festival features arts and crafts and a carnival area for small children. Discounts are available for tickets bought in advance. Included in the festival is a Wurstfest 10K Walk and the Wurstfest Art Show.

Hours

Mon. – Fri. . . . . 5 pm – 11 pm
Saturdays . . . . 11 am – 1 am
Sundays . . . . 11 am – 10 pm

Cost for Adults $6
Children under 12 . . . . Free

Directions

The festival takes place inside Landa Park. Take I-35 North and exit Walnut. Go left for two miles until Walnut intersects with Landa Street. Go right two blocks to the entrance of Landa Park. The festival will be on the left, shortly after entering the park.